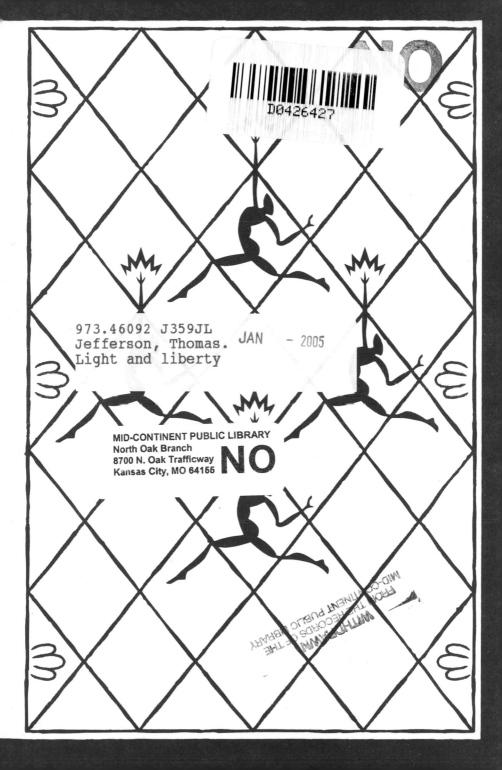

THOMAS JEFFERSON

LIGHT

AND

LIBERTY

REFLECTIONS ON THE PURSUIT
OF HAPPINESS

Edited by Eric S. Petersen

THE MODERN LIBRARY

NEW YORK

2004 Modern Library Edition

Compilation, preface, chronology, and notes copyright © 2004 by Eric S. Petersen

LIBRARY OF CONGRESS CATALOGING-IN-PUBLICATION DATA
Petersen, Eric S.
Light and liberty : reflections on the pursuit of happiness/edited by Eric S. Petersen.
p.   cm.
"Collections of essays pieced together from 700 individual phrases found in
Jefferson's writings"—CIP data sheet.
ISBN 0-679-64311-7
1. Jefferson, Thomas, 1743–1826—Quotations. 2. Conduct of life—Quotations,
maxims, etc. I. Jefferson, Thomas, 1743–1826. Selections. 2004. II. Title.

E302.J442 2004
973.46'092—dc22
[B]   2003044283

Modern Library website address: www.modernlibrary.com

Printed in the United States of America on acid-free paper

2 4 6 8 9 7 5 3

At Jefferson's Taper

He who receives an idea from me, receives instruction himself without lessening mine; as he who lights his taper at mine, receives light without darkening me. That ideas should freely spread from one to another over the globe, for the moral and mutual instruction of man, and improvement of his condition, seems to have been peculiarly and benevolently designed by nature, when she made them, like fire, expansible over all space, without lessening their density in any point, and like the air in which we breathe, move, and have our physical being, incapable of confinement or exclusive approbation.

—Thomas Jefferson to Isaac McPherson, 1813

CONTENTS

PREFACE

Thomas Jefferson was the foremost voice of the great patriots who consolidated the victory of the American Revolution, the leader most trusted to articulate our national ideals, particularly in times of trial and transition. His Declaration of American Independence, Virginia Statute for Religious Freedom, and First Inaugural Address can confidently be placed among the world's most powerful and admired inspirational essays. Under Jefferson's steady hand, the hopeful promise of the Revolution was transformed into the permanent reality of a continental republic based on Enlightenment principles. The creation, stabilization, and preservation of the United States of America was so central to his existence that he once called the American government the idol of his soul.

Thomas Jefferson's excellence as a writer was a highly effective weapon in his public battles. He repeatedly captured the high ground in contests of opinion by producing writings so compelling, so expressive of what the American people really felt and wanted, that they effectively curtailed debate. When Jefferson died on July 4, 1826, his political legacy included a huge quantity of official papers which he wrote during the time he held six elective and three appointive public offices (delegate to the Continental Congress, Virginia state representative, Virginia Governor, U.S. Representative, Minister to France, Secretary of State, Vice President and President of the United States, and Father of the University of Virginia). Among them are public addresses, official communications, reports, statutes, pamphlets, observations, replies, travel journals, biographical sketches, and a multitude of other writings vast and varied in character.

Jefferson also left to his family and ultimately to the world a voluminous collection of personal correspondence, always incisive and frequently profound. With characteristic discipline and foresight, he copied and preserved nearly 20,000 letters, using the ingenious copying gadgetry that so delighted him. His letters were composed for family, friends, colleagues, and even strangers, whose constant flood of correspondence he could not refuse to answer. Always occupied in the public service, the only book Thomas Jefferson wrote was *Notes on the State of Virginia,* an engaging and widely read description of various aspects of his native state suffused with observations on human progress.

Soon after my youthful joy in Jefferson was rekindled by a dear friend and fellow Jefferson admirer, I was fortunate to come into possession of a substantially complete collection of Jefferson's works. It was a mint collection of the Lipscomb and Bergh edition, assembled at the turn of the twentieth century, when the American public's appreciation of Jefferson was ascending on the trajectory that ultimately led to the creation in 1943 of the Jefferson Memorial in Washington, D.C. In that simpler and more freely patriotic time, what in the Revolutionary era was called genuine public approbation flowed freely and generously toward Thomas Jefferson. Citizens and civic leaders alike expressed their gratitude for his contributions to our nation without

reservation or qualification. They bought subscriptions for the purchase from private hands of Jefferson's Monticello home and regu-
larly made speeches of tribute to his leadership and achievements.

It is difficult to come away from a reading of Jefferson's complete
writings without being struck by his elevated perspective, and feeling
thankful for his life. As I entered into and began to absorb his en-
nobling thought, it gradually became clear to me how lofty Jefferson's
standards were, for us as individuals and for America as a nation, and
how fulfilling it would be if in our present pursuit of happiness we
could strive to attain those standards. This book is my attempt to bring
the light of Thomas Jefferson back into the American sky.

Jefferson had unbounded love for America, and through his words
the heart of our country speaks. America, the hallowed ark of human
hope and happiness. America, the depository of the sacred fire of freedom and self-government. America, the land of steady character, love
of liberty, and obedience to law. America, where the equal rights of
man and the happiness of every individual are acknowledged to be the
only legitimate objects of government. America, the great experiment
which was to prove that man is capable of living in society, governing
itself by laws self-imposed, and securing to its members the enjoyment of life, liberty, and the pursuit of happiness. In poetic prose,
Thomas Jefferson gives perpetual life to what he called the holy spirit
of 1776.

Jefferson's etchings of the American character are unique, and they
never lose their capacity to inspire. It is in our nature, he wrote, to invent and execute, to find means within ourselves, and not to lean on
others. To contract a habit of industry and activity. To be assiduous
in learning, take much exercise for health, and practice much virtue.
To become honest and useful to our fellow man. To consider nothing
as desperate, and surmount every difficulty with resolution and contrivance. To try all things, and hold fast that which is good. To fear no

injury any man can do us. To render cheerfully any service in our
power, of whatever description. To lose no opportunity to exercise
our hearts in benevolence. To act according to the dictates of our own
reason. To follow truth, justice, and plain dealing. To let common
sense and common honesty have fair play. To tolerate with utmost
latitude the right of others to differ. To take religion as a matter between our Maker and ourselves. To establish a character of liberality
and magnanimity. To be grateful, to be faithful to all engagements
under all circumstances, and to be open and generous. To have nothing to do with conquest. To let the love of our country soar above all
minor passions.

The concept for the structure of this book takes a cue from Jefferson's own "The Life and Morals of Jesus of Nazareth, Extracted Textu-
ally from the Gospels, in Greek, Latin, French and English." Jefferson
felt that the simple facts of Jesus' life, and the actual words Jesus
spoke, were the truly valuable parts of the Bible. So, initially as a late-
night activity in the space of a week during his first term as President
and later as one of his many retirement projects, he cut apart the
Gospels of Matthew, Mark, Luke, and John in four languages, elimi-
nated duplications, and arranged the snippets in a plausible order. The
resulting short tract, kept private for personal use during his lifetime,
was found among Jefferson's papers following his death. In print today,
it bears the title *The Jefferson Bible*. As in all things essentially Jeffersonian, simplicity and sagacity triumph.

Light and Liberty likewise seeks to set forth Thomas Jefferson's own
wisdom in a succinct and useful form. A scan of the source notes will
quickly suggest how it was compiled. Each segment is a composite of
five to thirty-three separate quotations, selected mostly from Jefferson's letters, and from some public documents, written over a period
of more than half a century. The words thus are entirely his. I have
merely arranged them, each as a single writing organized under a

virtue or good quality, in a way which concentrates their inspirational power. The personal nature of the material emanates from its origins largely in his correspondence. My effort to create smoothly flowing text, to the extent it has been successful, is attributable to the remarkable consistency of Jefferson's style and philosophy expressed over the course of his long life.

It has wisely been observed that the reader invites the consciousness of the writer. Thomas Jefferson's consciousness flowed from the highest plane. He lived not just for his momentous times but for all time. He wrote not just for his friends in life but for you and me, his friends in posterity. His words and wisdom are an unparalleled legacy. Thomas Jefferson illumined the pathway of world progress to a brighter future. His vision of light and liberty will ever remain the vision America cherishes.

LIGHT
AND
LIBERTY

FAITH

. . . Adore God . . .

I have ever thought religion a concern purely between our God and our consciences, for which we were accountable to Him, and not to the priests. I never told my own religion, nor scrutinized that of another. I never attempted to make a convert, nor wished to change another's creed. I have ever judged of the religion of others by their lives, for it is in our lives, and not from our words, that our religion must be read. By the same test the world must judge me.

Hitherto I have been under the guidance of that portion of reason which He has thought proper to deal out to me. I have followed it faithfully in all important cases, to such a degree at least as leaves me without uneasiness; and if on minor occasions I have erred from its dictates, I have trust in Him who made us what we are, and know it was not His plan to make us always unerring.

Faith and works will show their worth by their weight in the scales of eternal justice before God's tribunal. If no action is to be deemed virtuous for which malice can imagine a sinister motive, then there never was a virtuous action; no, not even in the life of our Saviour himself. But He has taught us to judge the tree by its fruit and to leave motives to Him who can alone see into them. There is only one God and He is all perfect. There is a future state of rewards and punishments. To love God with all thy heart and thy neighbor as thyself, is the sum of religion.

I hold (without appeal to revelation) that when we take a view of the universe, in all its parts, general or particular, it is impossible for the human mind not to perceive and feel a conviction of design, consummate skill, and indefinite power in every atom of its composition. The movements of the heavenly bodies, so exactly held in their course by the balance of centrifugal and centripetal forces; the structure of our earth itself, with its distribution of lands, waters, and atmosphere; animal and vegetable bodies, examined in all their minutest particles; insects, mere atoms of life, yet as perfectly organized as man or mammoth; the mineral substances, their generation and uses; it is impossible, I say, for the human mind not to believe, that there is in all this, design, cause, and effect, up to an ultimate cause, a fabricator of all things from matter and motion, their preserver and regulator while permitted to exist in their present forms, and their regeneration into new and other forms.

When great evils happen, I am in the habit of looking out for what good may arise from them as consolations to us, and Providence has in fact so established the order of things, as that most evils are the means of producing some good. We are not in a world ungoverned by the laws and the power of a Superior Agent. Our efforts are in His hand, and directed by it; and He will give them their effect in His own time.

Our next meeting must be in a country for us not now very distant. For this journey we shall need neither gold nor silver in our purse, nor scrip, nor coats, nor staves. Nor is the provision for it more easy than the preparation has been kind. Nothing proves more than this, that the Being who presides over the world is essentially benevolent.

Adore God; reverence and cherish your parents; love your neighbor as yourself, and your country more than life. Be just; be true; murmur not at the ways of Providence—and the life into which you have entered will be one of eternal and ineffable bliss.

HAPPINESS

... Any Service in My Power ...

Be assiduous in learning, take much exercise for your health, and practice much virtue. Health, learning, and virtue, will insure your happiness; they will give you a quiet conscience, private esteem, and public honor. Beyond these, we want nothing but physical necessaries, and they are easily obtained.

Happiness is the aim of life. Virtue is the foundation of happiness. Utility is the test of virtue. If the wise be the happy man, as the sages say, he must be virtuous too; for, without virtue, happiness cannot be. Interesting occupations are essential to happiness. Indeed, the whole art of being happy consists in the art of finding employment. A mind always employed is always happy. This is the true secret, the grand recipe, for felicity. The idle are the only wretched. The Giver of life gave it for happiness and not for wretchedness.

All men are endowed by their Creator with inherent and inalienable rights; among these, are life, liberty, and the pursuit of happiness. Perfect happiness, I believe, was never intended by the Deity to be the lot of one of His creatures in this world; but that He has very much put in our power the nearness of our approaches to it, is what I have steadfastly believed.

Nothing makes me more happy than to render any service in my power, of whatever description. There are minds which can be pleased by honors and preferments; but I see nothing in them but envy and enmity. It is only necessary to possess them, to know how little they contribute to happiness, or rather how hostile they are to it. Honesty, disinterestedness, and good nature are indispensable to procure the esteem and confidence of those with whom we live, and on whose esteem our happiness depends.

Entertaining a due sense of our equal right to the use of our own faculties, to the acquisitions of our own industry, to honor and confidence from our fellow citizens, resulting not from birth but from our actions, and their sense of them; enlightened by a benign religion, professed, indeed, and practiced in various forms, yet all of them inculcating honesty, truth, temperance, gratitude, and the love of man; acknowledging an adoring and overruling Providence, which by all its dispensations proves that it delights in the happiness of man here and his greater happiness hereafter; with all these blessings, what more is necessary to make us a prosperous and happy people?

A constitution has been acquired, which, though neither of us thinks perfect, yet both consider as competent to render our fellow citizens the happiest and securest on whom the sun has ever shone. The only orthodox object of the institution of government is to secure the greatest degree of happiness possible to the general mass of those associated under it.

How soon the labor of men would make a paradise of the whole earth, were it not for misgovernment, and a diversion of all his energies from their proper object—the happiness of man,—to the selfish interests of kings, nobles, and priests. If we can prevent the government from wasting the labors of the people, under the pretense of taking care of them, they must become happy. We who have gone before have performed an honest duty, by putting in the power of our successors a state of happiness which no nation ever before had within their choice.

If, in my retirement to the humble station of a private citizen, I am accompanied with the esteem and approbation of my fellow citizens, trophies obtained by the blood-stained steel, or the tattered flags of the tented field, will never be envied. The care of human life and happiness, and not their destruction, is the first and only legitimate object of good government. We wish the happiness and prosperity of every nation.

It will give me the greatest pleasure, and our whole family joins in the invitation, if, consulting your own conscience and comfort, you would make as long a stay at Monticello as time should permit. You know our course of life. To place our friends at their ease we show them that we are so ourselves, by pursuing the necessary vocations of the day and enjoying their company at the usual hours of society. Is it impossible to hope that this unexplored country may tempt your residence by holding out materials wherewith to build a fame, founded on the happiness and not the calamities of human nature?

I am as happy nowhere else, and in no other society, and all my wishes end, where I hope my days will end, at Monticello. God send you a safe deliverance, a happy issue out of all afflictions, personal and public, with long life, long health, and friends as sincerely attached as yours affectionately. I sincerely supplicate Heaven that your own personal welfare may long make a part of the general prosperity of a great, a free, and a happy people. The religion you so sincerely profess tells us we shall meet again; and we have all lived so as to be assured it will be in happiness.

ASPIRATION

. . . Practice the Purest Virtue . . .

Nothing can contribute more to your future happiness (moral rectitude always excepted), than the contracting a habit of industry and activity. Of all the cankers of human happiness none corrodes with so silent, yet so baneful an influence as indolence. Body and mind both unemployed, our being becomes a burden, and every object about us loathsome, even the dearest. Idleness begets ennui, ennui the hypochondriac, and that a diseased body. No laborious person was ever yet hysterical. I am constantly roving about to see what I have never seen before, and shall never see again.

Our greatest happiness does not depend on the condition of life in which chance has placed us, but is always the result of a good conscience, good health, occupation, and freedom in all just pursuits. The precept is wise which directs us to try all things, and hold fast that which is good. Nothing is troublesome that we do willingly. In endeavors to improve our situation, we should never despair. Be not weary of well doing. Let the eye of vigilance never be closed. Become an honest and useful man to those among whom we live. Above all things be good, because without that we can neither be valued by others nor set any value on ourselves.

Encourage all your virtuous dispositions, and exercise them whenever an opportunity arises; being assured that they will gain in strength by exercise, as a limb of the body does, and that exercise will make them habitual. From the practice of the purest virtue, you may be assured you will derive the most sublime comforts in every moment of life, and in the moment of death. The relations which exist between man and his Maker, and the duties resulting from those relations, are the most interesting and important to every human being, and the most incumbent on his study and investigation. I never go to bed without an hour, or half hour's, previous reading of something moral, whereon to ruminate in the intervals of sleep. Whether I retire to bed early or late I am up with the sun.

Of those recorded by historians few incidents have been attended with such circumstances as to excite in any high degree this sympathetic emotion of virtue. We are, therefore, wisely framed to be as warmly interested for a fictitious as for a real personage. The field of imagination is thus laid open to our use and lessons may be formed to illustrate and carry home to the heart every moral rule of life. Thus a lively and lasting sense of filial duty is more effectually impressed on the mind of a son or daughter by reading *King Lear*, than by all the dry volumes of ethics, and divinity that were ever written. This is my idea of well written Romance, of Tragedy, Comedy, and Epic poetry.

It is part of the American character to consider nothing as desperate; to surmount every difficulty with resolution and contrivance. When we see ourselves in a situation which must be endured and gone through, it is best to make up our minds to it. Meet it with firmness and accommodate everything to it in the best way practicable. This lessens the evil, while fretting and fuming only serves to increase our own torment. Fortitude teaches us to meet and surmount difficulties; not to fly from them, like cowards; and to fly, too, in vain, for they will meet and arrest us at every turn of our road. Go on therefore with courage and you will find it grows easier and easier.

I most cordially sympathize in your late immediate losses. It is a situation in which a man needs the aid of all his wisdom and philosophy. But as it is better to turn from the contemplation of our misfortunes to the resources we possess of extricating ourselves, you will, of course, have found solace in your vigor of mind, health of body, talents, habits of business, in the consideration that you have time yet to retrieve everything, and a knowledge that the very activity necessary for this, is a state of greater happiness than the unoccupied one, to which you had a thought of retiring.

You tell me my granddaughter repeated to you an expression of mine, that I should be willing to go again over the scenes of past life. I should not be unwilling, without, however wishing it; and why not? I have enjoyed a greater share of health than falls to the lot of most men; my spirits have never failed me except under those paroxysms of grief which you, as well as myself, have experienced in every form, and with good health and good spirits, the pleasures surely outweigh the pains in life. Why not, then, taste them again, fat and lean together?

Fitness

... The Sovereign Invigorator ...

Without health there is no happiness. An attention to health, then, should take the place of every other object. The time necessary to secure this by active exercises, should be devoted to it, in preference to every other pursuit. I know the difficulty with which a studious man tears himself from his studies, at any given moment of the day. But his happiness, and that of his family depend on it. The most uninformed mind, with a healthy body, is happier than the wisest valetudinarian. Knowledge indeed is a desirable, a lovely possession, but I do not scruple to say that health is more so. In my view, no knowledge can be more satisfactory to a man than that of his own frame, its parts, their functions and actions.

Take a great deal of exercise and on foot. Of all exercises walking is the best. A horse gives but a kind of half exercise, and a carriage is no better than a cradle. No one knows, till he tries, how easily a habit of walking is acquired. A person who never walked three miles will in the course of a month be able to walk fifteen or twenty without fatigue. I have known some great walkers, and had particular accounts of many more; and I never knew or heard of one who was not healthy or long lived. Love of repose will lead, in its progress, to a suspension of healthy exercise, a relaxation of mind, an indifference to everything around you, and finally to a debility of body, and hebetude of mind, the farthest of all things from happiness.

Never think of taking a book with you. The object of walking is to relax the mind. You should, therefore, not permit yourself even to think while you walk; but divert yourself by the objects surrounding you. A little walk of half an hour, in the morning, when you first arise, is advisable. It shakes off sleep, and produces other good effects in the animal economy. Rise at a fixed and early hour, and go to bed at a fixed and early hour also. Sitting up late at night is injurious to the health, and not useful to the mind.

The weather should be little regarded. A person not sick will not be injured by getting wet. Brute animals are the most healthy, and they are exposed to all weather and, of men, those are healthiest who are the most exposed. The recipe of these two descriptions of beings is simple diet, exercise, and the open air, be its state what it will; and we may venture to say that this recipe will give health and vigor to every other description. The sun is my almighty physician.

Having been so often a witness to the salutary efforts which nature makes to re-establish the disordered functions, the judicious, the moral, the human physician should rather trust to their action, than hazard the interruption of that, and a greater derangement of the system, by conjectural experiments on a machine so complicated and unknown as the human body, and a subject so sacred as human life.

I have lived temperately, eating little animal food, and that not as an aliment, so much as a condiment for the vegetables which constitute my principal diet. Ardent wines I cannot drink, nor do I use ardent spirits in any form. I have for fifty years bathed my feet in cold water every morning, and having been remarkably exempted from colds (not having had one in every seven years of my life on an average), I have supposed it might be ascribed to that practice. I enjoy good health; too feeble, indeed, to walk much, but riding without fatigue six or eight miles a day, and sometimes thirty or forty. The loss of the power of taking exercise would be a sore affliction to me. It has been the delight of my retirement to be in constant bodily activity, looking after my affairs. The sovereign invigorator of the body is exercise.

CHEERFULNESS

... Sweeten the Temper ...

Exercise and application produce order in our affairs, health of body, and cheerfulness of mind, and these make us precious to our friends. Husband well your time, cherish your instructors, strive to make everybody your friend. All the world will love you if you continue good humored, prudent, and attentive to everybody, as I am sure you will do from temper as well as reflection. Life is of no value but as it brings us gratifications. Among the most valuable of these is rational society. It informs the mind, sweetens the temper, cheers our spirits, and promotes health.

I estimate the qualities of the mind; 1, good humor; 2, integrity; 3, industry; 4, science. The preference of the first to the second quality may not at first be acquiesced in; but certainly we had all rather associate with a good-humored, light-principled man, than with an ill-tempered rigorist in morality. Good humor is one of the preservatives of our peace and tranquility. It is among the most effectual, and its effect is so well imitated and aided, artificially, by politeness, that this also becomes an acquisition of first rate value. Nothing enables a man to get along in business so well as a smooth temper.

I have been too much the butt of falsehoods myself to do others the injustice of permitting them to make the least impression on me. Though I have made up my mind not to suffer calumny to disturb my tranquility, yet I retain all my sensibilities for the approbation of the good and just. That is, indeed, the chief consolation for the hatred of so many, who, without the least personal knowledge, cover me with their implacable hatred. The only return I will ever make them, will be to do them all the good I can, in spite of their teeth. I do not agree that an age of pleasure is no compensation for a moment of pain. I think, with you, that life is a fair matter of account, and the balance often, nay generally, in its favor.

It is a happy circumstance in human affairs, that evils which are not cured in one way will cure themselves in some other. No man has greater confidence than I have, in the spirit of the people, to a rational extent. Whatever they can, they will. I cannot act as if all men were unfaithful because some are so; nor believe that all will betray me, because some do. I had rather be the victim of occasional infidelities, than relinquish my general confidence in the honesty of man.

Our administration now drawing towards a close, I have a sublime pleasure in believing that it will be distinguished as much by having placed itself above all the passions which could disturb its harmony, as by the great operations by which it will have advanced the well-being of the nation. That others may be found whose talents and integrity render them proper deposits of the public liberty and interests, and who have made themselves known by their eminent services, we can all affirm, of our personal knowledge. Our ship is sound, the crew alert at their posts, and our ablest steersman at its helm. That she will make a safe port I have no doubt; and that she may, I offer to heaven my daily prayers.

Contemplating the union of sentiment now manifested so generally, as auguring harmony and happiness to our future course, I offer to our country sincere congratulations. Our wish, as well as theirs, is, that the public efforts may be directed honestly to the public good, that peace may be cultivated, civil and religious liberty unassailed, law and order preserved, equality of rights maintained, and that state of property, equal or unequal, which results to every man from his own industry, or that of his fathers.

I yield the concerns of the world with cheerfulness to those who are appointed in the order of nature to succeed to them. I pray you to re-member, that should any occasion offer wherein I can be useful to you, there is no one on whose friendship and zeal you may more confi-dently count. Should it be in my power to render any service, I shall do it with cheerfulness.

GRATITUDE

... Among the Most Inestimable of Our Blessings ...

Called upon to undertake the duties of the first executive office of our country, I avail myself of the presence of that portion of my fellow citizens which is here assembled, to express my grateful thanks for the favor with which they have been pleased to look toward me, to declare a sincere consciousness that the task is above my talents, and that I approach it with those anxious and awful presentiments which the greatness of the charge and the weakness of my powers so justly inspire.

When we assemble together to consider the state of our beloved country, our just attentions are first drawn to those pleasing circumstances which mark the goodness of that Being from whose favor they flow, and the large measure of thankfulness we owe for His bounty. Among the most inestimable of our blessings is that of liberty to worship our Creator in the way we think most agreeable to His will; a liberty deemed in other countries incompatible with good government and yet proved by our experience to be its best support.

I have but one system of ethics for men and for nations—to be grateful, to be faithful to all engagements and under all circumstances, to be open and generous, promoting in the long run even the interests of both; and I am sure it promotes their happiness. While we devoutly return thanks to the Beneficent Being who has been pleased to breathe into our sister nations the spirit of conciliation and forgiveness, we are bound with peculiar gratitude to be thankful to Him that our own peace has been preserved.

Among the felicities which have attended my administration, I am most thankful for having been able to procure coadjutors so able, so disinterested, and so harmonious. Scarcely ever has a difference of opinion appeared among us which has not, by candid consultation, been amalgamated into something which all approved; and never one which in the slightest degree affected our personal attachments. The proof we have lately seen of the innate strength of our government, is one of the most remarkable which history has recorded, and shows that we are a people capable of self-government, and worthy of it.

It is wise and well to be contented with the good things which the Master of the feast places before us, and to be thankful for what we have, rather than thoughtful about what we have not. Lose no occasion of exercising your dispositions to be grateful, to be generous, to be charitable, to be humane, to be true, just, firm, orderly, and courageous. Consider every act of this kind as an exercise which will strengthen your moral faculties and increase your worth.

Everything is useful which contributes to fix in the principles and practices of virtue. When any original act of charity or of gratitude, for instance, is presented either to our sight or imagination, we are deeply impressed with its beauty and feel a strong desire in ourselves of doing charitable and grateful acts also.

I thank you, fellow-citizens, for the solicitude you kindly express for my future welfare. A retirement from the exercise of my present charge is equally for your good and my happiness. Gratitude for past favors, and affectionate concern for the liberty and prosperity of my fellow-citizens, will cease but with life to animate my breast.

SINCERITY

... Sentiments Long and Radically Mine ...

I am made very happy by learning that the sentiments expressed in my inaugural address gave general satisfaction, and holds out a ground on which our fellow citizens can once more unite. I am the more pleased, because these sentiments have been long and radically mine, and therefore will be pursued honestly and conscientiously.

I would be glad to know when any individual member of Congress thinks I have gone wrong in any instance. If I know myself, it would not excite ill blood in me, while it would assist to guide my conduct, perhaps to justify it, and to keep me to my duty, alert. Should my views of the subject be even wrong, I am sure they will find their apology with you in the purity of the motives of personal and public regard which induce a suggestion of them.

I know but one code of morality for men, whether acting singly or collectively. He who says I will be a rogue when I act in company with a hundred others, but an honest man when I act alone, will be believed in the former assertion, but not in the latter. Honesty is the first chapter in the Book of Wisdom. Let it be our endeavor to merit the character of a just nation.

The exact truth should be told. They will believe the good, if we candidly tell them the bad also. Honesty promotes interest in the long run. I can conscientiously declare that as to myself, I wish that not only no act but no thought of mine should be unknown.

The succession to Doctor Franklin, at the court of France, was an excellent school of humility. On being presented to any one as the minister of America, the commonplace question used in such cases was "C'est vous, Monsieur, qui remplace le Docteur Franklin?" I generally answered, "No one can replace him, sir; I am only his successor."

I hope I may be allowed to say that my public proceedings were always directed by a single view to the best interests of our country. I meddled in no intrigues, pursued no concealed object. I disdained all means which were not as open and honorable, as their object was pure. The whole art of government consists in the art of being honest. Only aim to do your duty, and mankind will give you credit where you fail. Let common sense and common honesty have fair play and they will soon set things to rights.

I have received letters expressed in the most friendly and even affectionate terms, sometimes, perhaps asking my opinion on some subject. I cannot refuse to answer such letters, nor can I do it dryly and suspiciously. Among a score or two of such correspondents, one perhaps betrays me. I feel it mortifyingly, but conclude I had better incur one treachery than offend a score or two of good people. I sometimes expressly desire that my letter may not be published; but this is so like requesting a man not to steal or cheat, that I am ashamed of it after I have done it.

Sincerity I value above all things; as, between those who practice it, falsehood and malice work their efforts in vain. I disdain everything like duplicity. Good faith is every man's surest guide. Of you, my neighbors, I may ask, in the face of the world, "Whose ox have I taken, or whom have I defrauded? Whom have I oppressed, or of whose hand have I received a bribe to blind mine eyes therewith?" On your verdict I rest with conscious security.

Not Thirsting for Gain

...Hands As Clean As They Are Empty...

When I first entered on the stage of public life, I came to a resolution never to engage while in public office in any kind of enterprise for the improvement of my fortune, nor to wear any other character than that of a farmer. I have never departed from it in a single instance. Thus I have thought myself richer in contentment than I should have been with any increase of fortune.

No man ever had less desire of entering into public offices than myself. In truth, I wish for neither honors nor offices. I am happier at home than I can be elsewhere. I have no ambition to govern men; no passion which would lead me to delight to ride in a storm. Whenever a man has cast a longing eye on offices, a rottenness begins in his conduct. I love to see honest and honorable men at the helm, men who will not bend their politics to their purses, nor pursue measures by which they may profit, and then profit by their measures. I have the consolation of having added nothing to my private fortune, during my public service, and of retiring with hands as clean as they are empty.

The glow of one warm thought is to me worth more than money. It is neither wealth nor splendor, but tranquility and occupation, which give happiness. Wealth, title, and office are no recommendations to my friendship. On the contrary, great good qualities are requisite to make amends for their having wealth, title, and office. I have not observed men's honesty to increase with their riches. In the great work which has been effected in America, no individual has a right to take any great share to himself.

Greediness for wealth, and fantastical expense, have degraded, and will degrade, the minds of our citizens. These are the peculiar vices of commerce. The selfish spirit of commerce knows no country, and feels no passion or principle but that of gain. Would a missionary appear, who would make frugality the basis of his religious system, and go through the land, preaching it up as the only road to salvation, I would join his school, though not generally disposed to seek my religion out of the dictates of my own reason, and feelings of my own heart.

I have never been so well pleased, as when I could shift power from my own, on the shoulders of others; nor have I ever been able to conceive how any rational being could propose happiness to himself from the exercise of power over others. I have seen enough of political honors to know that they are but splendid torments. The little spice of ambition which I had in my younger days has long since evaporated, and I set still less store by a posthumous than present name. Pride costs us more than hunger, thirst, and cold.

Never did a prisoner, released from his chains, feel such relief as I shall on shaking off the shackles of power. Nature intended me for the tranquil pursuits of science, by rendering them my supreme delight. But the enormities of the times in which I have lived, have forced me to take a part in resisting them, and to commit myself on the boisterous ocean of political passions. I thank God for the opportunity of retiring from them without censure, and carrying with me the most consoling proofs of public approbation.

SEEING THE GOOD

... The Honor of His Own, and the Model of Future Times ...

On James Monroe: You have formed a just opinion of Monroe. He is a man whose soul might be turned wrong side outwards, without discovering a blemish to the world.

On Benjamin Franklin: Dr. Franklin was the greatest man and ornament of the age and country in which he lived, and the father of American philosophy. No one of the present age has made more important discoveries, nor has enriched philosophy with more, or more ingenious solutions of the phenomena of nature. His memory will be preserved and venerated as long as the thunder of heaven shall be heard or feared.

On Alexander Hamilton: Hamilton was indeed a singular character. Of acute understanding, disinterested, honest, and honorable in all private transactions, amiable in society, and duly valuing virtue in private life, yet so bewitched and perverted by the British example, as to be under thorough conviction that corruption was essential to the government of a nation.

On George Mason: George Mason was a man of the first order of wisdom among those who acted on the theater of the Revolution, of expansive mind, profound judgment, cogent in argument, learned in the lore of our former constitution, and earnest for the republican change on democratic principles. His elocution was neither flowing nor smooth; but his language was strong, his manner most impressive, and strengthened by a dash of biting cynicism when provocation made it seasonable.

On Dabney Carr: His character was of a high order. A spotless integrity, sound judgment, handsome imagination, enriched by education and reading, quick and clear in his conceptions, of correct and ready elocution, impressing every hearer with the sincerity of the heart from which it flowed. His firmness was inflexible in whatever he thought was right; but when no moral principle stood in the way, never had man more of the milk of human kindness, of indulgence, of softness, of pleasantry of conversation and conduct. The number of his friends and the warmth of their affection, were proofs of his worth, and of their estimate of it.

On David Rittenhouse: We have supposed Mr. Rittenhouse second to no astronomer living; that in genius he must be the first, because he is self taught. As an artist he has exhibited as great a proof of mechanical genius as the world has ever produced. He has not indeed made a world; but he has by imitation approached nearer its Maker than any man who has lived from the creation to this day.

On George Wythe: No man ever left behind him a character more venerated than George Wythe. His virtue was of the purest tint; his integrity inflexible and his justice exact; of warm patriotism, and, devoted as he was to liberty, and the natural and equal rights of man, he might truly be called the Cato of his country, without the avarice of the Roman; for a more disinterested person never lived. Temperance and regularity in all his habits, gave him general good health, and his unaffected modesty and suavity of manners endeared him to everyone. He was of easy elocution, his language chaste, methodical in the arrangement of his matter, learned and logical in the use of it, and of great urbanity in debate; not quick of apprehension, but, with a little time, profound in penetration, and sound in conclusion. In his philosophy he was firm, and neither troubling, nor perhaps trusting, any one with his religious creed, he left the world to the conclusion, that religion must be good which could produce a life of such exemplary virtue. Such was George Wythe, the honor of his own, and the model of future times.

On George Washington: I think I knew General Washington intimately and thoroughly; and were I called on to delineate his character, it should be in terms like these: His mind was great and powerful without being of the very first order; his penetration strong, though not so acute as that of Newton, Bacon, or Locke; and, as far as he saw, no judgment was ever sounder. He was incapable of fear, meeting personal danger with the calmest unconcern. Perhaps the strongest feature of his character was prudence, never acting until every circumstance, every consideration, was maturely weighed; refraining if he saw a doubt, but, when once decided, going through with his purpose, whatever obstacles opposed. His integrity was most pure, his justice the most inflexible I have ever known, no motives of interest or consanguinity, of friendship or hatred, being able to bias his decision. He was, indeed, in every sense of the words, a wise, a good, and a great man. On the whole, his character was, in its mass, perfect, in nothing bad, in few points indifferent; and it may truly be said, that never did nature and fortune combine more perfectly to make a man great, and to place him in the same constellation with whatever worthies have merited from man an everlasting remembrance.

On Samuel Adams: I can say that Samuel Adams was truly a great man, wise in council, fertile in resources, immovable in his purposes, and had, I think, a greater share than any other member, in advising and directing our measures, in the Northern war. As a speaker, he could not be compared with his living colleague and namesake, whose deep conceptions, nervous style, and undaunted firmness, made him truly our bulwark in debate. But Mr. Samuel Adams, although not of fluent elocution, was so rigorously logical, so clear in his views, abundant in good sense, and master always of his subject, that he commanded the most profound attention, whenever he rose in an assembly, by which the froth of declamation was heard with the most sovereign contempt.

On Ontassete: I knew much the great Ontassete, the warrior and orator of the Cherokees; he was always the guest of my father, on his journeys to and from Williamsburg. I was in his camp when he made his great farewell oration to his people the evening before his departure for England. The moon was in full splendor, and to her he seemed to address himself in his prayers for his own safety on the voyage, and that of his people during his absence; his sounding voice, distinct articulation, animated action, and the solemn silence of his people at their several fires, filled me with awe and veneration, although I did not understand a word he uttered.

On Peyton Randolph: He was indeed a most excellent man; and none was ever more beloved and respected by his friends. Somewhat cold and coy towards strangers, but of the sweetest affability when ripened into acquaintance. Of Attic pleasantry in conversation, always good humored and conciliatory. With a sound and logical head, he was well read in the law; and his opinions, when consulted, were highly regarded, presenting always a learned and sound view of subject. In criminal prosecutions exaggerating nothing, he aimed at a candid and just state of the transaction, believing it more a duty to save an innocent than to convict a guilty man. Although not eloquent, his matter was so substantial that no man commanded more attention, which, joined with a sense of his great worth, gave him a weight in the House of Burgesses which few ever attained.

On Meriwether Lewis: My message to Congress proposed the sending an exploring party to trace the Missouri to its source, to cross the highlands and follow the best water communication which offered itself from thence to the Pacific Ocean. Congress approved the proposition, and voted a sum of money for carrying it into execution. Captain Lewis, who had then been near two years with me as private secretary, immediately renewed his solicitations to have the direction of the party. I had now had opportunities of knowing him intimately. Of courage undaunted, possessing a firmness and perseverance of purpose which nothing but impossibilities could divert from its direction, careful as a father of those committed to his charge, yet steady in the maintenance of order and discipline, intimate with the Indian character, customs, and principles. Habituated to the hunting life, guarded by exact observation of the vegetables and animals of his own country, against losing time in the description of objects already possessed, honest, disinterested, liberal, of sound understanding, and a fidelity to truth so scrupulous that whatever he should report would be as certain as if seen by ourselves, with all these qualifications as if selected and implanted by nature in one body, for this express purpose, I could have no hesitation in confiding the enterprise to him.

On James Madison: Trained in the successive schools of the Legislature of Virginia and Congress, he acquired a habit of self-possession, which placed at ready command the rich resources of his luminous and discriminating mind, and of his extensive information, and rendered him the first of every assembly afterwards, of which he became a member. Never wandering from his subject into vain declamation, but pursuing it closely, in language pure, classical, and copious, soothing always the feelings of his adversaries by civilities and softness of expression, he rose to the eminent station which he held in the great National Convention of 1787; and in that of Virginia which followed, he sustained the new Constitution in all its parts, bearing off the palm against the logic of George Mason, and the fervid declamation of Mr. Henry. With these consummate powers, were united a pure and spotless virtue, which no calumny has ever attempted to sully. Of the powers and polish of his pen, and of the wisdom of his administration in the highest office of the nation, I need say nothing. They have spoken, and will forever speak for themselves.

JESUS

... Morals Most Perfect and Sublime ...

Jesus appeared. His parentage was obscure; his condition poor; his education null; his natural endowments great; his life correct and innocent; he was meek, benevolent, patient, firm, disinterested, and of the sublimest eloquence. He pushed his scrutinies into the heart of man; erected his tribunal in the region of his thoughts, and purified the waters at the fountain head. A system of morals is presented to us, which, if filled up in the style and spirit of the rich fragments he left us, would be the most perfect and sublime that has ever been taught by man. According to the ordinary fate of those who attempt to enlighten and reform mankind, he fell an early victim to the jealousy and combination of the altar and the throne.

We find in the writings of His biographers matter of two distinct descriptions. First, a groundwork of vulgar ignorance, of things impossible, of superstitions, fanaticisms, and fabrications. Intermixed with these, again, are sublime ideas of the Supreme Being, aphorisms, and precepts of the purest morality and benevolence, sanctioned by a life of humility, innocence, and simplicity of manners, neglect of riches, absence of worldly ambition and honors, with an eloquence and persuasiveness which have not been surpassed.

The practice of morality being necessary for the well-being of society, He has taken care to impress its precepts so indelibly on our hearts that they shall not be effaced by the subtleties of our brain. We all agree in the obligation of the moral precepts of Jesus, and nowhere will they be found delivered in greater purity than in His discourses. I have made a wee-little book, which I call *The Philosophy of Jesus;* it is a paradigma of His doctrines, made by cutting the text out of the Gospels of Matthew, Mark, Luke, and John, and arranging them on the pages of a blank book, in a certain order of time or subject. A more beautiful or precious morsel of ethics I have never seen.

When we shall have knocked down the artificial scaffolding, reared to mask from view the simple structure of Jesus; when, in short, we shall have unlearned everything which has been taught since His day, and got back to the pure and simple doctrines He inculcated, we shall then be truly and worthily His disciples; and my opinion is that if nothing had ever been added to what flowed purely from His lips, the whole world would at this day have been Christian.

The mild and simple principles of the Christian philosophy would produce too much calm, too much regularity of good, to extract from its disciples a support from a numerous priesthood, were they not to sophisticate it, ramify it, split it into hairs, and twist its texts till they cover the divine morality of its author with mysteries, and require a priesthood to explain them. The Quakers seem to have discovered this. They have no priests, therefore no schisms. They judge of the text by the dictates of common sense and common morality. It is a matter of principle with me to avoid disturbing the tranquility of others by the expression of any opinion on the innocent questions on which we schismatize. Religious animosities I impute to those who call themselves His ministers, and who engraft their casuistries on the stock of His simple precepts. I am sometimes more angry with them than is authorized by the blessed charities which He preaches.

As to myself, my religious reading has long been confined to the moral branch of religion, which is the same in all religions; while in that branch which consists of dogmas, all differ, all have a different set. The former instructs us how to live well and worthily in society; the latter are made to interest our minds in the support of the teachers who inculcate them. I am a Christian, in the only sense in which He wished anyone to be; sincerely attached to his doctrines, in preference to all others; ascribing to himself every human excellence; and believing he never claimed any other.

NATURE'S BEAUTY

... So Rich a Mantle ...

Lake George, New York. Lake George is, without comparison, the most beautiful water I ever saw; formed by a contour of mountains into a basin thirty-five miles long, and from two or four miles broad, finely interspersed with islands, its water limpid as crystal, and the mountain sides covered with rich groves of thuja, silver fir, white pine, aspen, and paper birch down to the water-edge; here and there precipices of rock to checker the scene and save it from monotony.

Potomac and Shenandoah River Junction, Virginia. The passage of the Potomac through the Blue Ridge is, perhaps, one of the most stupendous scenes in nature. You stand on a very high point of land. On your right comes up the Shenandoah, having ranged along the foot of the mountain an hundred miles to seek a vent. On your left approaches the Potomac, in quest of a passage also. In the moment of their junction, they rush together against the mountain, rend it asunder, and pass off to the sea. But the distant finishing which nature has given to the picture, is of a very different character. It is a true contrast to the foreground. It is as placid and delightful as that is wild and tremendous. For the mountain being cloven asunder, she presents to your eye, through the cleft, a small catch of smooth blue horizon, at an infinite distance in the plain country, inviting you as it were from the riot and tumult roaring around to pass through the breach and participate of the calm below.

Heidelberg, Germany. Heidelberg is on the Neckar just where it issues from the Bergstrasse mountains, occupying the first skirt of plain which it forms. The chateau is up the hill a considerable height. The gardens lie above the chateau, climbing up the mountain in terraces. This chateau is the most noble ruin I have ever seen, having been reduced to that state by the French in the time of Louis XIV., 1693. Nothing remains under cover but the chapel. The situation is romantic and pleasing beyond expression. The apple, the pear, cherry, peach, apricot, and almond, are all in bloom. There is a station in the garden to which the chateau re-echoes distinctly four syllables.

The Natural Bridge, Rockbridge County, Virginia. The Natural Bridge, the most sublime of nature's works, is on the ascent of a hill, which seems to have been cloven through its length by some great convulsion. The fissure, just at the bridge, is, by some admeasurements, 270 feet deep, by others only 205. Its breadth in the middle is about 60 feet, but more at the ends, and the thickness of the mass, at the summit of the arch, about 40 feet. A part of this thickness is constituted by a coat of earth, which gives growth to many large trees. The residue, with the hill on both sides, is one solid rock of lime-stone. Though the sides of this bridge are provided in some parts with a parapet of fixed rocks, yet few men have resolution to walk to them, and look over into the abyss. You involuntarily fall on your hands and feet, creep to the parapet, and peep over it. Looking down from this height about a minute, gave me a violent head-ache. If the view from the top be painful and intolerable, that from below is delightful in an equal extreme. It is impossible for the emotions arising from the sublime to be felt beyond what they are here; so beautiful an arch, so elevated, so light, and springing as it were up to heaven! The rapture of the spectator is really indescribable!

Monticello at Charlottesville, Virginia. And our own dear Monticello— where has Nature spread so rich a mantle under the eye?—Mountains, forests, rocks, rivers. With what majesty do we ride above the storms! How sublime to look down into the workhouse of Nature, to see her clouds, hail, snow, rain, thunder, all fabricated at our feet! And the glorious sun, when rising as if out of a distant water, just gliding the tops of the mountains, and giving life to all nature!

Humility

... All Are Perfectly Equal ...

In America no other distinction between man and man had ever been known, but that of persons in office, exercising powers by authority of the laws, and private individuals. Among these last, the poorest laborer stood on equal ground with the wealthiest millionaire, and generally on a more favored one, whenever their rights seemed to jar. It has been seen that a shoemaker or other artisan, removed by the voice of his country from his work-bench into a chair of office, has instantly commanded all the respect and obedience which the laws ascribe to his office. But of distinction by birth or badge, they had no more idea than they had of the mode of existence in the moon or planets. They had heard only that there were such, and knew that they must be wrong.

I can further say, with safety, there is not a crowned head in Europe, whose talents or merits would entitle him to be elected a vestryman, by the people of any parish in America. The new government has shown genuine dignity, in my opinion, in exploding adulatory titles; they are the offerings of abject baseness, and nourish that degrading vice in the people. When brought together in society, all are perfectly equal, whether foreign or domestic, titled or untitled, in or out of office. The fool has as great a right to express his opinion by vote as the wise, because he is equally free, and equally master of himself.

The rights of conscience we never submitted, we could not submit. We are answerable for them to our God. The legitimate powers of government extend to such acts only as are injurious to others. It does me no injury for my neighbor to say there are twenty gods, or no God. It neither picks my pocket nor breaks my leg. Is this then our freedom of religion? And are we to have a censor whose imprimatur shall say what books may be sold, and what we may buy? And who is thus to dogmatize religious opinions for our citizens? Whose foot is to be the measure to which ours are all to be cut or stretched?

Having been one of those who entered into public life at the commencement of an era the most extraordinary which the history of man has ever yet presented to his contemplation, I claim nothing more, for the part I have acted in it, than a common merit of having, with others, faithfully endeavored to do my duty in the several stations allotted me. I have been connected, as many fellow laborers were, with the great events which happened to mark the epoch of our lives. But these belong to no one in particular, all of us did our parts, and no one can claim the transactions to himself.

Your statements of the corrections of the Declaration of Independence by Dr. Franklin and Mr. Adams are neither of them at all exact. I should think it better to say generally that the rough draft was communicated to those two gentlemen, who each of them made two or three short and verbal alterations only, but even this is laying more stress on mere composition than it merits, for that alone was mine. The sentiments were of all America.

Disapproving myself of transferring the honors and veneration for the great birthday of our Republic to any individual, or of dividing them with individuals, I have declined letting my own birthday be known, and have engaged my family not to communicate it. This has been the uniform answer to every application of the kind.

SACRIFICE

...A Debt of Service Is Due from Every Man...

A recollection of our former vassalage in religion and civil government, will unite the zeal of every heart, and the energy of every hand, to preserve that independence in both which, under the favor of Heaven, a disinterested devotion to the public cause first achieved, and a disinterested sacrifice of private interests will now maintain.

The supremacy of the civil over the military authority; economy in the public expense, that labor may be lightly burdened; the honest payment of our debts and sacred preservation of the public faith; encouragement of agriculture, and of commerce as its handmaid; the diffusion of information and the arraignment of all abuses at the bar of public reason; freedom of religion; freedom of the press; freedom of person under the protection of the habeas corpus; and trial by juries impartially selected—these principles form the bright constellation which has gone before us, and guided our steps through an age of revolution and reformation. The wisdom of our sages and the blood of our heroes have been devoted to their attainment. They should be the creed of our political faith—the text of civil instruction—the touchstone by which to try the services of those we trust; and should we wander from them in moments of error or alarm, let us hasten to retrace our steps and to regain the road which alone leads to peace, liberty, and safety.

A debt of service is due from every man to his country, proportioned to the bounties which nature and fortune have measured to him. It is for the public interest to encourage sacrifices and services, by rewarding them, and they should weigh to a certain point, in the decision between candidates. In a virtuous government, and more especially in times like these, public offices are, what they should be, burdens to those appointed to them, which it would be wrong to decline, though foreseen to bring with them intense labor, and great private loss.

A person who wishes to make the gift of office an engine for self-elevation, may do wonders with it; but to one who wishes to use it conscientiously for the public good, without regard to the ties of blood or friendship, it creates enmities without numbers, many open, but more secret, and saps the happiness of his life. To the sacrifice of time, labor, fortune, a public servant must count upon adding that of peace of mind, and even reputation.

I have been for some time used as the property of the newspapers, a fair mark for every man's dirt. Some, too, have indulged themselves in this exercise who would not have done it, had they known me otherwise than through these impure and injurious channels. It is hard treatment, and for a singular kind of offense, that of having obtained by the labors of a life the indulgent opinions of a part of one's fellow citizens. However, these moral evils must be submitted to, like the physical scourges of tempest, fire, etc. Politics, like religion, holds up the torches of martyrdom to the reformers of error.

Possessed of the blessing of self-government, and of such a portion of civil liberty as no other civilized nation enjoys, it now behooves us to guard and preserve them by a continuance of the sacrifices and exertions by which they were acquired, and especially to nourish that Union which is their sole guarantee. We owe every sacrifice to ourselves, and to the world at large, to pursue with temper and perseverance the great experiment which shall prove that man is capable of living in society, governing itself by laws self-imposed, and securing to its members the enjoyment of life, liberty, property, and peace. The last hope of human liberty in this world rests on us. We ought, for so dear a state, to sacrifice every attachment and every enmity. If ever there was a holy war, it was that which saved our liberties and gave us independence.

The approbation of my ancient friends is, above all things, the most grateful to my heart. They know for what objects we relinquished the delights of domestic society, tranquility, and science, and committed ourselves to the ocean of revolution, to wear out the only life God has given us here in scenes the benefits of which will accrue only to those who follow us.

I have ever found in my progress through life, that, acting for the public, if we do always what is right, the approbation denied in the beginning will surely follow us in the end. It is from posterity we are to expect remuneration for the sacrifices we are making for their service, of time, quiet, and good will.

Being True to Yourself

...This Faithful Internal Monitor...

Nature has written her moral laws on the head and heart of every rational and honest man, where every man may read them for himself. If ever you are about to say anything amiss, or to do anything wrong, consider beforehand you will feel something within you which will tell you it is wrong, and ought not to be said or done. This is your conscience, and be sure and obey it. Our Maker has given us all this faithful internal monitor, and if you always obey it you will always be prepared for the end of the world; or for a much more certain event, which is death. This must happen to all; it puts an end to the world as to us; and the way to be ready for it is never to do a wrong act. Conscience is the only sure clue which will eternally guide a man clear of all doubts and inconsistencies.

I am of a sect by myself, as far as I know. When I am led by conversation to express my sentiments, I do it with the same independence here which I have practiced everywhere, and which is inseparable from my nature. I never submitted the whole system of my opinions to the creed of any party of men whatever, in religion, in philosophy, in politics, in anything else, where I was capable of thinking for myself. Such an addiction, is the last degradation of a free and moral agent. If I could not go to heaven but with a party, I would not go there at all.

From the moment that a portion of my fellow citizens looked towards me with a view to one of their highest offices, the floodgates of calumny have been opened upon me; not where I am personally known, where their slanders would be instantly judged and suppressed, from a general sense of their falsehood; but in the remote parts of the Union, where the means of detection are not at hand, and the trouble of an inquiry is greater than would suit the hearers to undertake. I know that I might have filled the courts of the United States with actions for these slanders, and have ruined perhaps many persons who are not innocent. But this would be no equivalent to the loss of character. I leave them, therefore, to the reproof of their own consciences. If these do not condemn them, there will yet come a day when the false witness will meet a judge who has not slept over his slanders. No reformation can be hoped where there is no repentance.

Resort is had to ridicule only when reason is against us. Every man's own reason must be his oracle. Be assured that these little returns into ourselves, this self-catechizing habit, is not trifling nor useless, but leads to the prudent selection and steady pursuit of what is right. Man, once surrendering his reason, has no remaining guard against absurdities the most monstrous, and like a ship without rudder, is the sport of every wind. With such persons, gullibility, which they call faith, takes the helm from the hand of reason, and the mind becomes a wreck.

Is uniformity attainable? Millions of innocent men, women, and children, since the introduction of Christianity, have been burnt, tortured, fined, imprisoned; yet we have not advanced one inch toward uniformity. What has been the effect of coercion? To make one half the world fools, and the other half hypocrites. To support roguery and error all over the earth. Force cannot give right.

Mysticisms constitute the craft, the power, and the profit of the priests. Sweep away their gossamer fabrics of factitious religion, and they would catch no more flies. We should all then, like the Quakers, live without an order of priests, moralize for ourselves, follow the oracle of conscience, and say nothing about what no man can understand, nor therefore believe; for I suppose belief to be the assent of the mind to an intelligible proposition.

It behooves every man who values liberty of conscience for himself, to resist invasions of it in the case of others, or their case may, by change of circumstances, become his own; and to give no example of concession, betraying the common right of independent opinion, by answering questions of faith, which the laws have left between God and himself.

I never will, by any word or act, bow to the shrine of intolerance or admit a right of inquiry into the religious opinions of others. On the contrary, we are bound, you, I, and every one, to make common cause, even with error itself, to maintain the common right of freedom of conscience.

All this, my friend, is offered, merely for your consideration and judgment, without presuming to anticipate what you alone are qualified to decide for yourself.

SELF-PERFECTION

... The High Ground of Your Own Merits ...

Be very select in the society you attach yourself to, avoid taverns, drinkers, smokers, idlers, and dissipated persons generally; for it is with such that broils and contentions arise; and you will find your path more easy and tranquil.

When I recollect that at fourteen years of age, the whole care and direction of myself was thrown on myself entirely, without a relation or friend qualified to advise or guide me, and recollect the various sorts of bad company with which I associated from time to time, I am astonished I did not turn off with some of them, and become as worthless to society as they were. I had the good fortune to become acquainted very early with some characters of very high standing, and to feel the incessant wish that I could ever become what they were. Under temptations and difficulties, I would ask myself what would Dr. Small, Mr. Wythe, Peyton Randolph do in this situation? What course in it will insure me their approbation?

A determination never to do wrong, prudence, and good humor, will go far towards securing to you the estimation of the world. Go on deserving applause, and you will be sure to meet with it; and the way to deserve it is to be good, and to be industrious. Do not be discouraged by small difficulties; make it as perfect as you can at a first essay, and depend on amending its defects as they develop themselves in practice. Practice in this as in all other cases, will render that very easy which now appears to you of insuperable difficulty. Experience alone brings skill.

It will be found that crooked schemes will end by overwhelming their authors and coadjutors in disgrace, and that he alone who walks strict and upright, and who, in matters of opinion, will be contented that others should be as free as himself, and acquiesce when his opinion is fairly overruled, will attain his object in the end. Take from man his selfish propensities, and he can have nothing to seduce him from the practice of virtue. Or subdue those propensities by education, instruction, or restraint, and virtue remains without a competitor. Bold, unequivocal virtue is the best handmaid even to ambition. Nature has constituted utility to man, the standard and test of virtue.

The want or imperfection of the moral sense in some men, like the want or imperfection of the senses of sight and hearing in others, is no proof that it is a general characteristic of species. When it is wanting, we endeavor to supply the defect by education, by appeals to reason and calculation. You may give pain where perhaps you wish it, but be assured that it will re-act on yourself with double though delayed effect, and that it will be one of those incidents of your life on which you will never reflect with satisfaction. Be advised, then; stand erect before the world on the high ground of your own merits, without stooping to what is unworthy of notice.

The uniform tenor of a man's life furnishes better evidence of what he has said or done on any particular occasion than the word of any enemy, and of an enemy too, who shows that he prefers the use of falsehoods which suit him to truths which do not. I never did, or countenanced, in public life, a single act inconsistent with the strictest good faith; having never believed there was one code of morality for a public, and another for a private man. There is not a truth existing which I fear, or would wish unknown to the whole world.

DOING WHAT IS RIGHT

... Truth, Justice, and Plain Dealing ...

If ever you find yourself environed with difficulties and perplexing circumstances, out of which you are at a loss how to extricate yourself, do what is right, and be assured that will extricate you the best out of the worst situations. Though you cannot see, when you take one step, what will be the next, yet follow truth, justice, and plain dealing, and never fear their leading you out of the labyrinth, in the easiest manner possible. The knot which you thought a Gordian one, will untie itself before you. Nothing is so mistaken as the supposition that a person is to extricate himself from a difficulty by intrigue, by chicanery, by dissimulation, by trimming, by an untruth, by an injustice. This increases the difficulties tenfold; and those, who pursue these methods, get themselves so involved at length, that they can turn no way but their infamy becomes more exposed.

Give up money, give up fame, give up science, give up the earth itself and all it contains, rather than do an immoral act. And never suppose, that in any possible situation, or under any circumstances, it is best for you to do a dishonorable thing, however slightly so it may appear to you. Whenever you are to do a thing, though it can never be known but to yourself, ask yourself how you would act were all the world looking at you, and act accordingly. The precept of Providence is, to do always what is right, and leave the issue to Him.

It is of great importance to set a resolution, not to be shaken, never to tell an untruth. There is no vice so mean, so pitiful, so contemptible; and he who permits himself to tell a lie once, finds it much easier to do it a second and third time, till at length it becomes habitual; he tells lies without attending to it, and truths without the world's believing him. This falsehood of the tongue leads to that of the heart, and in time depraves all its good dispositions. Honesty which proceeds from the heart as well as the head may be more surely counted on.

Return with joy to that state of things, when the only questions concerning a candidate shall be, is he honest? Is he capable? Is he faithful to the Constitution? Every honest man will suppose honest acts to flow from honest principles, and the rogues may rail without intermission. Our part is to pursue with steadiness what is right, turning neither to the right nor left for the intrigues or popular delusions of the day, assured that the public approbation will in the end be with us.

I sincerely believe in the general existence of a moral instinct. I think it is the brightest gem with which the human character is studded, and the want of it as more degrading than the most hideous of the bodily deformities.

I shall expect from your justice that you will be equally ready to correct as to commit an error. It is not he who prints, but he who pays for printing a slander, who is its real author. Where wrong has been done, he who knows and conceals the doer of it, makes himself an accomplice, and justly censurable as such.

The right of opinion shall suffer no invasion from me. Those who have acted well have nothing to fear, however they may have differed from me in opinion: those who have done ill, however, have nothing to hope; nor shall I fail to do justice lest it should be ascribed to that difference of opinion. For even if we differ in principle more than I believe we do, you and I know too well the texture of the human mind, and the slipperiness of human reason, to consider differences of opinion otherwise than differences of form or feature. Integrity of views more than their soundness, is the basis of esteem.

Simplicity

...All Pith...

I am for a government rigorously frugal and simple. The accounts of the United States ought to be, and may be made as simple as those of a common farmer, and capable of being understood by common farmers. The people through all the States are for republican forms, republican principles, simplicity, economy, religious and civil freedom.

Our predecessors have endeavored by intricacies of system, and shuffling the investigator over from one officer to another, to cover everything from detection. I hope we shall go in the contrary direction, and that by our honest and judicious reformations, we may be able, within the limits of our time, to bring things back to that simple and intelligible system on which they should have been organized at first. Let us deserve well of our country by making her interests the end of all our plans, and not our own pomp, patronage, and irresponsibility.

Congress will pretty completely fulfill all the desires of the people. They have reduced the army and navy to what is barely necessary. They are disarming executive patronage and preponderance, by putting down one-half the offices of the United States, which are no longer necessary. These economies have enabled them to suppress all the internal taxes, and still to make such provision for the payment of their public debt as to discharge that in eighteen years. They are opening the doors of hospitality to fugitives from the oppressions of other countries; and we have suppressed all those public forms and ceremonies which tended to familiarize the public eye to the harbingers of another form of government.

The Senate and Representatives differed about the title of the President. The former wanted to style him "His Highness, George Washington, President of the United States, and Protector of their liberties." The latter insisted and prevailed, to give no title but that of office, to wit, "George Washington, President of the United States." I hope the terms of Excellency, Honor, Worship, Esquire, forever disappear from among us, from that moment: I wish that of Mr. would follow them.

I served with General Washington in the legislature of Virginia, before the revolution, and, during it, with Dr. Franklin in Congress. I never heard either of them speak ten minutes at a time, nor to any but the main point, which was to decide the question. They laid their shoulders to the great points, knowing that the little ones would follow of themselves. Speeches of sententious brevity, using not a word to spare, leave not a moment for inattention to the hearer. Amplification is the vice of modern oratory. It is an insult to an assembly of reasonable men, disgusting and revolting instead of persuading. Speeches measured by the hour, die with the hour.

In style, I have aimed at accuracy, brevity, and simplicity. No style of writing is so delightful as that which is all pith, which never omits a necessary word, nor uses an unnecessary one. No writer has exceeded Paine in ease and familiarity of style, in perspicuity of expression, happiness of elucidation, and in simple and unassuming language. In this he may be compared with Dr. Franklin; and his Common Sense was, for a while, believed to have been written by Dr. Franklin.

I thought it would be useful, also, in all new draughts, to reform the style of the later British statutes, and of our own acts of Assembly, which, from their verbosity, their endless tautologies, their involutions of case within case, and parenthesis within parenthesis, and their multiplied efforts at certainty by *saids* and *aforesaids*, by *ors* and by *ands*, to make them more plain, do really render them more perplexed and incomprehensible, not only to common readers, but to the lawyers themselves.

Let things come to rights by the plain dictates of common sense rather than by the practice of any artifices. Honest simplicity is now prevailing in America, and worthy of being cherished.

I long to be in the midst of the children, and have more pleasure in their little follies than in the wisdom of the wise. I had rather be shut up in a very modest cottage, with my books, my family, and a few old friends, dining on simple bacon, and letting the world roll on as it liked, than to occupy the most splendid post, which any human power can give.

LIVING IN THE PRESENT

... Act upon Things As They Are ...

Our business is to march straight forward to the object which has occupied us for eight and twenty years, without either turning to the right or left. And when that is done, you and I may retire to the tranquility which our years begin to call for, and revise with satisfaction the efforts of the age we happened to be born in, crowned with complete success. In the hour of death we shall have the consolation to see established in the land of our fathers the most wonderful work of wisdom and disinterested patriotism that has ever yet appeared on the globe.

It can never be too often repeated, that the time for fixing every essential right on a legal basis is while our rulers are honest, and ourselves united. I am greatly anxious to hear that nine States accept our new Constitution. We must be contented to accept of its good, and to cure what is evil in it hereafter. It seems necessary for our happiness at home; I am sure it is so for our respectability abroad. The ground of liberty is to be gained by inches. We must be contented to secure what we can get, from time to time, and eternally press forward for what is yet to get.

Although our prospect is peace, our policy and purpose is to provide for defense by all those means to which our resources are competent. It is our duty still to endeavor to avoid war; but if it shall actually take place, no matter by whom brought on, we must defend ourselves. If our house be on fire, without inquiring whether it was fired from within or without, we must try to extinguish it. In that, I have no doubt, we shall act as one man.

I agree in an almost unlimited condemnation of retrospective laws. The few instances of wrong which they redress are so overweighed by the insecurity they draw over all property and even over life itself, and by the atrocious violations of both to which they lead that it is better to live under the evil than the remedy.

That our Creator made the earth for the use of the living and not of the dead; that those who exist not can have no use nor right in it, no authority or power over it; that one generation of men cannot foreclose or burden its use to another, which comes to it in its own right and by the same divine beneficence; that a preceding generation cannot bind a succeeding one by its laws or contracts; these deriving their obligation from the will of the existing majority, and that majority being removed by death, another comes in its place with a will equally free to make its own laws and contracts; these are axioms so self-evident that no explanation can make them plainer; for he is not to be reasoned with who says that non-existence can control existence, or that nothing can move something. Let us draw a veil over the dead, and hope the best for the living.

Rights and powers can only belong to persons, not to things, not to mere matter, unendowed with will. The dead are not even things. The particles of matter which composed their bodies, make part now of the bodies of other animals, vegetables, or minerals, of a thousand forms. To what then are attached the rights and powers they held while in the form of men? A generation may bind itself as long as its majority continues in life; when that has disappeared, another majority is in place, holds all the rights and powers their predecessors once held, and may change their laws and institutions to suit themselves. Nothing then is unchangeable but the inherent and unalienable rights of man.

Of the public transactions in which I have borne a part, I have kept no narrative with a view of history. A life of constant action leaves no time for recording. Our duty is to act upon things as they are, and make a reasonable provision for whatever they may be. Never put off till tomorrow what you can do today.

I hope you will have good sense enough to disregard those foolish predictions that the world is to be at an end soon. The Almighty has never made known to anybody at what time He created it; nor will He tell anybody when He will put an end to it, if He ever means to do it. As to preparations for that event, the best is for you always to be prepared for it. The only way to be so is, never say or do a bad thing. Nature will not give you a second life wherein to atone for the omissions of this.

There is a time for things; for advancing and for retiring; for a Sabbath of rest as well as for days of labor, and surely that Sabbath has arrived for one near entering on his 80th year. Tranquility is the summum bonum of that age. I wish now for quiet, to withdraw from the broils of the world, to soothe the enmities, and to die in the peace and goodwill of all mankind.

ENTHUSIASM

... Every Bud That Opens ...

A rising nation, spread over a wide and fruitful land, traversing all the seas with the rich productions of their industry, engaged in commerce with nations who feel power and forget right, advancing rapidly to destinies beyond the reach of mortal eye,—when I contemplate these transcendent objects, and see the honor, the happiness, and the hopes of this beloved country committed to the issue and the auspices of this day, I shrink from the contemplation, and humble myself before the magnitude of the undertaking.

We contemplate this rapid growth, and the prospect it holds up to us, not with a view to the injuries it may enable us to do to others in some future day, but to the settlement of this extensive country still remaining vacant within our limits, to the multiplications of men susceptible of happiness, educated in the love of order, habituated to self-government, and valuing its blessings above all price.

As the storm is now subsiding, and the horizon becoming serene, it is pleasant to consider the phenomenon with attention. We can no longer say there is nothing new under the sun. For this whole chapter in the history of man is new. The great extent of our republic is new. The mighty wave of public opinion which has rolled over it is new. But the most pleasing novelty is, its so quietly subsiding over such an extent of surface to its true level again. The order and good sense displayed in this recovery from delusion, and in the momentous crisis which lately arose, really bespeak a strength of character in our nation which augurs well for the duration of our republic; and I am much better satisfied now of its stability than I was before it was tried.

We shall have our follies without doubt. Some one or more of them will always be afloat. But ours will be the follies of enthusiasm, not of bigotry. Bigotry is the disease of ignorance, of morbid minds; enthusiasm of the free and buoyant. Education and free discussion are the antidotes of both. We are destined to be a barrier against the returns of ignorance and barbarism. The preservation of the holy fire is confided to us by the world, and the sparks which will emanate from it will ever serve to rekindle it in other quarters of the globe.

The work we are now doing is, I trust, done for posterity, in such a way that they need not repeat it. We shall delineate with correctness the great arteries of this great country. Those who come after us will extend the ramifications as they become acquainted with them, and fill up the canvas we begin. I rejoice when I hear of young men of virtue and talents worthy to receive, and likely to preserve the splendid inheritance of self-government, which we have acquired and shaped for them.

Although I do not, with some enthusiasts, believe that the human condition will ever advance to such a state of perfection as that there shall no longer be pain or vice in the world, yet I believe it susceptible of much improvement, and most of all, in matters of government and religion; and that the diffusion of knowledge among the people is to be the instrument by which it is to be effected.

Seven years ago, I embarked in an enterprise, the establishment of a University, which placed and keeps me still under the public eye. The call was imperious, the necessity most urgent, and the hazard of titubation less, by those seven years, than it now is. The institution is at length happily advanced to completion, and has been commenced under auspices as favorable as I could expect. I hope it will prove a blessing to my own State, and not unuseful perhaps to some others. At all hazards, and secured by the aid of my able coadjutors, I shall continue, while I am in being, to contribute to it whatever my weakened and weakening powers can.

I have often thought that if heaven had given me choice of my position and calling, it should have been on a rich spot of earth, well watered, and near a good market for the productions of the garden. No occupation is so delightful to me as the culture of the earth, and no culture comparable to that of the garden. Such a variety of subjects, some one always coming to perfection, the failure of one thing repaired by the success of another, and instead of one harvest a continued one through the year. Under a total want of demand except for our family table, I am still devoted to the garden. But though an old man, I am but a young gardener.

Botany I rank with the most valuable sciences, whether we consider its subjects as furnishing the principal subsistence of life to man and beast, delicious varieties for our tables, refreshments from our orchards, the adornments of our flower-borders, shade and perfume of our groves, materials for our buildings, or medicaments for our bodies. There is not a sprig of grass that shoots uninteresting to me, nor anything that moves.

The motion of my blood no longer keeps time with the tumult of the world. It leads me to seek for happiness in the lap and love of my family, in the society of my neighbors and my books, in the wholesome occupations of my farm and my affairs, in an interest or affection in every bud that opens, in every breath that blows around me, in an entire freedom of rest, of motion, of thought, owing account to myself alone of my hours and actions.

Patriotism

... The Sole Depository of the Sacred Fire ...

We are trusted with the destinies of this solitary republic of the world, the only monument of human rights, and the sole depository of the sacred fire of freedom and self-government, from hence it is to be lighted up in other regions of the earth, if other regions of the earth shall ever become susceptible of its benign influence. All mankind ought then, with us, to rejoice in its prosperous, and sympathize in its adverse fortunes, as involving everything dear to man. And to what sacrifices of interest, or convenience, ought not these considerations to animate us? To what compromises of opinion and inclination, to maintain harmony and union among ourselves, and to preserve from all danger this hallowed ark of human hope and happiness.

My earnest prayers to all my friends are to cherish mutual good will, to promote harmony and conciliation, and above all things to let the love of our country soar above all minor passions. To preserve the peace of our fellow citizens, promote their prosperity and happiness, reunite opinion, cultivate a spirit of candor, moderation, charity, and forbearance toward one another, are objects calling for the efforts and sacrifices of every good man and patriot. Our religion enjoins it; our happiness demands it; and no sacrifice is requisite but of passions hostile to both.

The first object of my heart is my own country, the asylum for whatever is great and good. In that is embarked my family, my fortune, and my own existence. I have not one farthing of interest, nor one fibre of attachment out of it, nor a single motive of preference of any one nation to another, but in proportion as they are more or less friendly to us. There is not a country on earth where there is greater tranquillity; where the laws are milder, or better obeyed; where every one is more attentive to his own business or meddles less with that of others; where strangers are better received, more hospitably treated, and with a more sacred respect; where the virtues of the heart are less exposed to be weakened.

A character of good faith is of as much value to a nation as to an individual. A nation, as a society, forms a moral person, and every member of it is personally responsible for his society. The man who loves his country on its own account, and not merely for its trappings of interest or power, can never be divorced from it, can never refuse to come forward when he finds that she is engaged in dangers which he has the means of warding off. To no events which can concern the future welfare of my country, can I ever become an indifferent spectator; her prosperity will be my joy, her calamities my affliction.

Nothing on earth is more certain, than that if myself particularly, placed by my office of Vice-President at the head of the republicans, had given way and withdrawn from my post, the republicans throughout the Union would have given up in despair, and the cause would have been lost forever. By holding on, we obtained time for the Legislature to come up with their weight; and those of Virginia and Kentucky particularly, by their celebrated resolutions, saved the Constitution at its last gasp. No person who was not a witness of the scenes of that gloomy period, can form any idea of the afflicting persecutions and personal indignities we had to brook. They saved our country, however.

Our fellow citizens have a sacred attachment to the event of which the paper of July 4th, 1776, was but the Declaration, the genuine effusion of the soul of our country at that time. Small things may, perhaps, like the relics of saints, help to nourish our devotion to this holy bond of our Union, and keep it longer alive and warm in our affections. Even should the cloud of barbarism and despotism again obscure the science and liberties of Europe, this country remains to preserve and restore light and liberty to them. In short, the flames kindled on the 4th of July, 1776, have spread over too much of the globe to be extinguished by the feeble engines of despotism; on the contrary, they will consume these engines and all who work them.

Looking forward with anxiety to the future destinies of my countrymen I trust that, in their steady character unshaken by difficulties, in their love of liberty, obedience to law, and support of the public authorities, I see a sure guarantee of the permanence of our Republic; and retiring from the charge of their affairs, I carry with me the consolation of a firm persuasion that Heaven has in store for our beloved country long ages to come of prosperity and happiness. God send to our country a happy deliverance.

LIBERTY

... Members of the Universal Society of Mankind ...

Every man, and every body of men on earth, possesses the right of self-government. They receive it with their being from the hand of nature. Individuals exercise it by their single will; collections of men by that of their majority; for the law of the majority is the natural law of every society of men.

All, too, will bear in mind this sacred principle, that though the will of the majority is in all cases to prevail, that will, to be rightful, must be reasonable; that the minority possess their equal rights, which equal laws must protect, and to violate which would be oppression. Let us, then, fellow citizens, unite with one heart and one mind.

In every government on earth is some trace of human weakness, some germ of corruption and degeneracy, which cunning will discover and wickedness insensibly open, cultivate, and improve. Every government degenerates when trusted to the rulers of the people alone. The people themselves, therefore, are its only safe depositaries. And to render even them safe, their minds must be improved to a certain degree.

I consider the people who constitute a society or nation as the source of all authority in that nation, as free to transact their common concerns by any agents they think proper, to change these agents individually, or the organization of them in form or function whenever they please; that all the acts done by those agents under the authority of the nation, are the acts of the nation, are obligatory on them, and enure to their use, and can in no wise be annulled or affected by any change in the form of the government, or of the persons administering it.

It should be remembered, as an axiom of eternal truth in politics, that whatever power in any government is independent, is absolute also; in theory only, at first, while the spirit of the people is up, but in practice, as fast as that relaxes. Independence can be trusted nowhere but with the people in mass. They are inherently independent of all but moral law.

The equal rights of man, and the happiness of every individual, are now acknowledged to be the only legitimate objects of government. Modern times have discovered the only device by which these rights can be secured, to wit; government by the people, acting not in person, but by representatives chosen by themselves, that is to say, by every man of right years and sane mind, who contributes either by his purse or person to the support of his country.

What has destroyed liberty and the rights of man in every government which has ever existed under the sun? The generalizing and concentrating all cares and powers into one body, no matter whether of the autocrats of Russia or France, or of the aristocrats of a Venetian senate. Indeed, it is difficult to conceive how so good a people as the French, with so good a King, so well-disposed rulers in general, so genial a climate, so fertile a soil, should be rendered so ineffectual for producing human happiness by one single curse,—that of a bad form of government. But it is a fact, in spite of the mildness of their governors, the people are ground to powder by the vices of the form of government. Of twenty millions of people supposed to be in France, I am of the opinion there are nineteen millions more wretched, more accursed in every circumstance of human existence than the most conspicuously wretched individual of the whole United States.

Our lot has been happier. When you witnessed our first struggles in the War of Independence, you little calculated, more than we did, on the rapid growth and prosperity of this country; on the practical demonstration it was about to exhibit, of the happy truth that man is capable of self-government, and only rendered otherwise by the moral degradation designedly superinduced on him by the wicked acts of his tyrants. If ever this vast country is brought under a single government, it will be one of the most extensive corruption, indifferent and incapable of a wholesome care over so wide a spread of surface. The time to guard against corruption and tyranny, is before they shall have gotten hold of us. It is better to keep the wolf out of the fold, than to trust to drawing his teeth and claws after he shall have entered.

I have much confidence that we shall proceed successfully for ages to come, and that, contrary to the principle of Montesquieu, it will be seen that the larger the extent of country, the more firm its republican structure, if founded, not on conquest, but in principles of compact and equality. My hope of its duration is built much on the enlargement of the resources of life going hand in hand with the enlargement of territory, and the belief that men are disposed to live honestly, if the means of doing so are open to them.

I considered as a great public acquisition the commencement of a settlement on the western coast of America and looked forward with gratification to the time when its descendants should have spread themselves through the whole length of that coast, covering it with free and independent Americans, unconnected with us but by the ties of blood and interest, and employing like us the rights of self-government. We should have such an empire for liberty as she has never surveyed since the creation; and I am persuaded no constitution was ever before so well calculated as ours for extensive empire and self-government.

We exist, and are quoted, as standing proofs that a government, so modeled as to rest continually on the will of the whole society, is a practicable government. Were we to break to pieces, it would damp the hopes and the efforts of the good, and give triumph to those of the bad through the whole enslaved world. As members, therefore, of the universal society of mankind, and standing in high and responsible relation with them, it is our sacred duty to suppress passion among ourselves, and not to blast the confidence we have inspired of proof that a government of reason is better than one of force.

It is indeed an animating thought, that while we are securing the rights of ourselves and our posterity, we are pointing out the way to struggling nations, who wish like us to emerge from their tyrannies also. Heaven help their struggles, and lead them, as it has done us, triumphantly through them. I join with you in the hope and belief that they will see, from our example, that a free government is of all others the most energetic; that the inquiry which has been excited among the mass of mankind by our revolution and its consequences, will ameliorate the condition of man over a great portion of the globe.

In Turkey, where the sole nod of the despot is death, insurrections are the events of every day. Compare again the ferocious depredations of their insurgents, with the order, the moderation, and the almost self-extinguishment of ours. And say, finally, whether peace is best preserved by giving energy to the government, or information to people. This last is the most certain, and the most legitimate engine of government. Educate and inform the whole mass of the people. Enable them to see that it is their interest to preserve peace and order, and they will preserve them. And it requires no very high degree of education to convince them of this. They are the only sure reliance for the preservation of our liberty.

The way to have good and safe government, is not to trust it all to one, but to divide it among the many, distributing to every one exactly the functions he is competent to. Let the national government be entrusted with the defense of the nation, and its foreign and federal relations; the state governments with the civil rights, laws, police, and administration of what concerns the state generally; the counties with the local concerns of the counties, and each ward direct the interests within itself. It is by dividing and subdividing these republics from the great national one down through all its subordinations, until it ends in the administration of every man's farm by himself; by placing under every one what his own eye may superintend, that all will be done for the best.

The article nearest my heart, is the division of counties into wards. These will be pure and elementary republics, the sum of all which, taken together, composes the state, and will make of the whole a true democracy as to the business of the wards, which is that of nearest and daily concern. The affairs of the larger sections, of counties, of states, and of the Union, not admitting personal transactions by the people, will be delegated to agents elected by themselves; and representation will thus be substituted, where personal action becomes impracticable. In this way we shall be as republican as a large society can be; and secure the continuance of purity in our government, by the salutary, peaceable, and regular control of the people.

To preserve the independence of the people, we must not let our rulers load us with perpetual debt. We must make our election between economy and liberty, or profusion and servitude. Considering the general tendency to multiply offices and dependencies, and to increase expense to the ultimate term of burden which the citizen can bear, may it never be seen here that, after leaving to labor the smallest portion of its earnings on which it can subsist, government shall itself consume the residue of what it was instituted to guard. To take from one, because it is thought that his own industry and that of his fathers has acquired too much, in order to spare to others, who, or whose fathers have not exercised equal industry and skill, is to violate arbitrarily the first principle of association, "the guaranty to every one of a free exercise of his industry, and the fruits acquired by it."

A bill of rights is what the people are entitled to against every government on earth, general or particular; and what no just government should refuse, or rest on inference. The Constitution should provide clearly, and without the aid of sophism, for freedom of religion, freedom of the press, protection against standing armies, restriction of monopolies, the eternal and unremitting force of the habeas corpus laws, and trials by jury in all matters of fact triable by the laws of land, and not by the laws of nations.

You seem to consider the judges as the ultimate arbiters of all constitutional questions; a very dangerous doctrine indeed, and one which would place us under the despotism of an oligarchy. Our judges are as honest as other men, and not more so. They have, with others, the same passions for party, for power, and the privilege of their corps. Their power is more dangerous, as they are in office for life, and not responsible, as the other functionaries are, to the elective control. The Constitution has erected no such single tribunal, knowing that to whatever hands confided, with the corrections of time and party, its members would become despots. It has more wisely made all the departments co-equal and co-sovereign within themselves.

In every country and in every age, the priest has been hostile to liberty. He is always in alliance with the despot, abetting his abuses in return for protection to his own. It is easier to acquire wealth and power by this combination than by deserving them, and to effect this, they have perverted the purest religion ever preached to man into mystery and jargon, unintelligible to all mankind, and therefore the safer engine for their purposes. History, I believe, furnishes no example of a priest-ridden people maintaining a free civil government. This marks the lowest grade of ignorance, of which their civil as well as religious leaders will always avail themselves for their own purposes. I have sworn upon the altar of God, eternal hostility against every form of tyranny over the mind of man. Rebellion to tyrants is obedience to God.

The eyes of the virtuous all over the earth are turned with anxiety on us, as the only depositaries of the sacred fire of liberty. I hope and firmly believe that the whole world will, sooner or later, feel benefit from the issue of our assertion of the rights of man. May the Declaration of Independence be to the world, what I believe it will be, (to some parts sooner, to others later, but finally to all,) the signal of arousing men to burst the chains under which monkish ignorance and superstition had persuaded them to bind themselves, and to assume the blessings and security of self-government. Cherish every measure which may foster our brotherly Union and perpetuate a constitution of government, destined to be the primitive and precious model of what is to change the condition of man over the globe.

Dreaming the Impossible

... Cast by the Favor of Heaven ...

Our Revolution commenced on favorable ground. It presented us an album on which we were free to write what we pleased. We had no occasion to search into musty records, to hunt up royal parchments, or to investigate the laws and institutions of a semi-barbarous ancestry. We appealed to those of nature, and found them engraved on our hearts. Ours was not only the first of the American States, but the first nation in the world, at least within the records of history, which peaceably by its wise men, formed on free deliberation, a constitution of government for itself, and deposited it in writing, among their archives, always ready and open to the appeal of every citizen.

Our lot has been cast by the favor of heaven in a country and under circumstances highly auspicious to our peace and prosperity, and where no pretense can arise for the degrading and oppressive establishments of Europe. It is our happiness that honorable distinctions flow only from public approbation; and that finds no object in titled dignitaries and pageants. Let us, then, endeavor carefully to guard this happy state of things, by keeping a watchful eye over the disaffection of wealth and ambition to the republican principles of our Constitution, and by sacrificing all our local and personal interests to the cultivation of the Union, and maintenance of the authority of the laws.

But the sufferings of all Europe will not be lost. A sense of the rights of man is gone forth, and all Europe will ere long have representative governments, more or less free. A first attempt to recover the right of self-government may fail, so may a second, a third, etc. But as a younger and more instructed race comes on, the sentiment becomes more and more intuitive, and a fourth, a fifth, or some subsequent one of the ever renewed attempts will ultimately succeed. For what inheritance so valuable, can man leave to his posterity? You and I shall look down from another world on these glorious achievements of man, which will add to the joys even of heaven.

In every country where man is free to think and to speak, differences of opinion will arise from differences of perception, and the imperfections of reason; but these differences when permitted, as in this happy country, to purify themselves by free discussion, are but as passing clouds overspreading our land transiently, and leaving our horizon more bright and serene.

I have observed this march of civilization advancing from the sea coast, passing over us like a cloud of light, increasing our knowledge and improving our condition, insomuch as that we are at this time more advanced in civilization here than the seaports were when I was a boy. And where this progress will stop no one can say. Barbarism has, in the meantime, been receding before the steady step of amelioration; and will in time, I trust, disappear from the earth.

All eyes are opened, or opening, to the rights of man. The general spread of the light of science has already laid open to every view the palpable truth, that the mass of mankind has not been born with saddles on their backs, nor a favored few booted and spurred, ready to ride them legitimately, by the grace of God. Mine, after all, may be a Utopian dream, but being innocent, I have thought I might indulge in it till I go to the land of dreams, and sleep there with the dreamers of all past and future times.

ONENESS

... Make Them One People ...

We feel that we are acting under obligations not confined to the limits of our own society. It is impossible not to be sensible that we are acting for all mankind; that circumstances denied to others, but indulged to us, have imposed on us the duty of proving what is the degree of freedom and self-government in which a society may venture to leave its individual members.

Our true interest will be best promoted by making all the just claims of our fellow citizens, wherever situated, our own; by urging and enforcing them with the weight of our whole influence; and by exercising in every instance a just government in their concerns, and making common cause even where our separate interest would seem opposed to theirs. No other conduct can attach us together; and on this attachment depends our happiness. I sincerely wish that the whole Union may accommodate their interests to each other, and play into their hands mutually as members of the same family, that the wealth and strength of any one part should be viewed as the wealth and strength of the whole.

It will be a great blessing to our country if we can once more restore harmony and social love among its citizens. I confess, as to myself, it is almost the first object of my heart, and one to which I would sacrifice everything but principle. With the people I have hopes of effecting it. The good sense of our people will direct the boat ultimately to its proper point.

The cement of this Union is in the heart-blood of every American. I do not believe there is on earth a government established on so im-movable a basis. By bringing the sects together and mixing with them, we shall soften their asperities, liberalize and neutralize their preju-dices, and make the general religion a religion of peace, reason, and morality. The greatest good we can do our country is to heal its party divisions, and make them one people.

Their arts, their science, and what they have left of virtue, will come over to us, and although their vices will come also, these, I think, will soon be diluted and evaporated in a country of plain honesty. Experi-ence will soon teach the new-comers how much more plentiful and pleasant is the subsistence gained by wholesome labor and fair deal-ing, than a precarious and hazardous dependence on the enterprises of vice and violence.

I sincerely pray that all the members of the human family may, in the time prescribed by the Father of us all, find themselves securely established in the enjoyment of life, liberty, and happiness. Every human being has an interest in the happiness and prosperity of every other. If it be possible to be certainly conscious of anything, I am conscious of feeling no difference between writing to the highest or lowest being on earth. The moral doctrines of Jesus of Nazareth inculcated universal philanthropy, not only to kindred and friends, but to all mankind, gathering all into one family, under the bonds of love, charity, peace, common wants, and common aids. No doctrines of Jesus lead to schism.

We are all created by the same Great Spirit; children of the same family. Why should we not live then as brothers ought to do? In that branch of religion which regards the moralities of life, and the duties of a social being, which teaches us to love our neighbors as ourselves, and to do good to all men, I am sure that you and I do not differ. He who steadily observes those moral precepts in which all religions concur, will never be questioned at the gates of heaven, as to the dogmas in which they all differ.

On entering the gate of heaven, we leave those badges of religious schism behind, and find ourselves united in those principles only in which God has united us all. Let us not be uneasy then about the different roads we may pursue, as believing them the shortest, to that our last abode; but, following the guidance of a good conscience, let us be happy in the hope that by these different paths we shall all meet in the end. And that you and I may there meet and embrace is my earnest prayer.

Hope

... The Dreams of the Future ...

We have acted together from the origin to the end of a memorable Revolution, and we have contributed, each in the line allotted us, our endeavors to render its issue a permanent blessing to our country. That our social intercourse may, to the evening of our days, be cheered and cemented by witnessing the freedom and happiness for which we have labored, will be my constant prayer.

We are likely to preserve the liberty we have obtained only by unremitting labors and perils. But we shall preserve it; and our mass of weight and wealth on the good side is so great, as to leave no danger that force will ever be attempted against us. I will not believe our labors are lost. I shall not die without a hope that light and liberty are on steady advance.

The spirit of 1776 is not dead. It has only been slumbering. The body of the American people is substantially republican. But their virtuous feelings have been played on by some fact with more fiction; they have been the dupes of artful maneuvers, and made for a moment to be willing instruments in forging chains for themselves. But time and truth have dissipated the delusion, and opened their eyes.

Our experience so far, has satisfactorily manifested the competence of a republican government to maintain and promote the best interests of its citizens; and every future year, I doubt not, will contribute to settle a question on which reason, and a knowledge of the character and circumstances of our fellow citizens, could never admit a doubt, and much less condemn them as fit subjects to be consigned to the dominion of wealth and force.

We shall never give up our Union, the last anchor of our hope, and that alone which is to prevent this heavenly country from becoming an arena of gladiators. Here we are pacifically inclined, if anything comes which will permit us to follow our inclinations. I hope we shall once more see harmony restored among our citizens, and an entire oblivion of past feuds. I will sacrifice everything but principle to procure it.

I indulge a single hope only, that the choice of President may fall on one who will be a friend of peace, of economy, of the republican principles of our Constitution, and of the salutary distribution of powers made by that between the general and the local governments. To promote, therefore, unanimity and perseverance in this great enterprise, to disdain despair, encourage trial, and nourish hope, are the worthiest objects of every political and philanthropic work. We, too, shall encounter follies; but if great, they will be short; if long, they will be light; and the vigor of our country will get the better of them. Should things go wrong at any time, the people will set them to rights by the peaceable exercise of their elective rights.

We are sincerely anxious to see mankind raised from their present abject condition. The light which has been shed on the mind of man through the civilized world, has given it a new direction, from which no human power can divert it. The sovereigns of Europe who are wise, or have wise counselors, see this, and bend to the breeze which blows; the unwise alone stiffen and meet its inevitable crush. The ball of liberty is now so well in motion that it will roll round the globe.

That every man shall be made virtuous, by any process whatever, is, indeed, no more to be expected, than that every tree shall be made to bear fruit, and every plant nourishment. The brier and bramble can never become the vine and olive; but their asperities may be softened by culture, and their properties improved to usefulness in the order and economy of the world. And I do hope that, in the present spirit of extending to the great mass of mankind the blessings of instruction, I see a prospect of great advancement in the happiness of the human race; and that this may proceed to an indefinite, although not to an infinite degree. Nature has sown talents and virtues as liberally among the poor as rich, and which are lost to their country by the want of means for their cultivation.

The reformation of offenders, though an object worthy of the attention of the laws, is not effected at all by capital punishments, which exterminate instead of reforming, and should be the last melancholy recourse against those whose existence is become inconsistent with the safety of their fellow citizens; which also weaken the State by cutting off so many who, if reformed, might be restored sound members to society, who, even under a course of correction, might be rendered useful in various labors for the public, and would be, living, and long-continued spectacles to deter others from committing the like offenses.

I had rather be deceived than live without hope. It is so sweet! It makes us ride so smoothly over the roughness of life. My theory has always been, that if we are to dream, the flatteries of hope are as cheap, and pleasanter than the gloom of despair.

When I contemplate the immense advances in science and discoveries in the arts which have been made within the period of my life, I look forward with confidence to equal advances by the present generation, and have no doubt that they will consequently be as much wiser than we have been as we than our fathers were, and they than the burners of witches.

Withdrawn by age from all other public services and attentions to public things, I am closing the last scenes of life by fashioning and fostering an establishment for the instruction of those who are to come after us. I hope its influence on their virtue, freedom, fame, and happiness, will be salutary and permanent. The form and distributions of its structure are original and unique, the architecture chaste and classical, and the whole well worthy of attracting the curiosity of a visit.

I like the dreams of the future better than the history of the past. That yourself, your family and people may repose at length in freedom, happiness, and safety, shall be our constant prayer and that God may ever have you, great and dear friend and ally, in His safe and holy keeping.

LIFE ACCEPTANCE

... Doing What Good We Can ...

The varieties in the structure and action of the human mind, as in those of the body, are the work of our Creator, against which it cannot be a religious duty to erect the standard of uniformity. I see too many proofs of the imperfection of human reason to entertain wonder or intolerance at any difference of opinion on any subject; and acquiesce in that difference as easily as on a difference of feature or form; experience having long taught me the reasonableness of mutual sacrifices of opinion among those who are to act together for any common object, and the expediency of doing what good we can, when we cannot do all we would wish.

I do not believe that fourteen out of fifteen men are rogues: I believe a great abatement from that portion may be made in favor of general honesty. But I have always found that rogues would be uppermost. Ignorance and bigotry, like other insanities, are incapable of self-government.

An association of men who will not quarrel with one another is a thing which never yet existed, from the greatest confederacy of nations down to a town meeting or a vestry. It seems that the smaller the society the bitterer the dissensions into which it breaks. I believe ours is to owe its permanence to its great extent, and the smaller portion comparatively, which can ever be convulsed at one time by local passions.

It is very difficult to persuade the great body of mankind to give up what they have once learned, and are now masters of, for something to be learnt anew. Time alone insensibly wears down old habits, and produces small changes at long intervals, and to this process we must all accommodate ourselves, and be content to follow those who will not follow us. If we keep together we shall be safe, and when error is so apparent as to become visible to the majority, they will correct it, and what we suffer during the error must be carried to account with the losses by tempests, earthquakes, etc.

The most fortunate of us, in our journey through life, frequently meet with calamities and misfortunes which may greatly afflict us; and, to fortify our minds against the attacks of these calamities and misfortunes, should be one of the principal studies and endeavors of our lives. The only method of doing this is to assume a perfect resignation to the Divine will, to consider that whatever does happen, must happen; and that, by our uneasiness, we cannot prevent the blow before it does fall, but we may add to its force after it has fallen. My principle is to do whatever is right, and leave the consequences to Him who has the disposal of them.

Deeply practiced in the school of affliction, the human heart knows no joy which I have not lost, no sorrow of which I have not drunk! Fortune can present no grief of unknown form to me! Who, then, can so softly bind up the wound of another, as he who has felt the same wound himself? To the question, indeed, on the utility of grief, no answer remains to be given. I see that, with the other evils of life, it is destined to temper the cup we are to drink.

The injury of which you had heard, was a dislocated wrist, and though it was a simple dislocation, and immediately aided by the best surgeon in Paris, it is neither well, nor ever will be, so as to render me much service. The fingers remain swelled and crooked, the hand withered, and the joint having a very confined motion. We have no rose without its thorn; no pleasure without alloy. It is the law of our existence; and we must acquiesce. It is the condition annexed to all our pleasures, not by us who receive, but by Him who gives them.

Man, like the fruit he eats, has his period of ripeness. Like that, too, if he continues longer hanging to the stem, it is but a useless and unsightly appendage. There is a fulness of time when men should go, and not occupy too long the ground to which others have a right to advance. I am now retired: I resign myself, as a passenger, with confidence to those at present at the helm, and ask but for rest, peace, and goodwill.

Dr. Franklin used to say that when he was young and had time to read he had not books; and now when he has become old and had books, he had no time. Perhaps it is that when habit has strengthened our sense of duties, they leave us no time for other things; but when young we neglect them and this gives us time for anything. Our machines have now been running seventy or eighty years, and we must expect that, worn as they are, here a pivot, there a wheel, now a pinion, next a spring, will be giving way; and however we may tinker them up for a while, all will at length surcease motion. Our watches, with works of brass and steel, wear out within that period.

I wish to offend no man's opinion, nor to draw disquieting animadversions on my own. While duty required it, I met opposition with a firm and fearless step. But loving mankind in my individual relations with them, I pray to be permitted to depart in their peace; and like the superannuated soldier, to hang my arms on the post.

When you and I look back on the country over which we have passed, what a field of slaughter does it exhibit! Where are all the friends who entered it with us, under all the inspiring energies of health and hope? As if pursued by the havoc of war, they are strewed by the way, some earlier, some later, and scarce a few stragglers remain to count the numbers fallen, and to mark yet, by their own fall, the last footsteps of their party. Is it a desirable thing to bear up through the heat of the action, to witness the death of all our companions, and merely be the last victim? I doubt it. We have, however, the traveler's consolation. Every step shortens the distance we have to go; the end of our journey is in sight, the bed wherein we are to rest, and to rise in the midst of the friends we have lost. "We sorrow not then as others who have no hope"; but look forward to the day which "joins us to the great majority."

SELF-GIVING

. . . Useful to the Cause of Humanity . . .

We acknowledge that our children are born free; that that freedom is the gift of nature, and not of him who begot them; that though under our care during infancy, and therefore of necessity under a duly tempered authority, that care is confided to us to be exercised for the preservation and good of the child only; and his labors during youth are given as a retribution for the charges of infancy.

God has formed us moral agents. Not that, in the perfection of His state, He can feel pain or pleasure in anything we may do; He is far above our power; but that we may promote the happiness of those with whom He has placed us in society, by acting honestly towards all, benevolently to those who fall within our way, respecting sacredly their rights, bodily and mental, and cherishing especially their freedom of conscience, as we value our own.

I believe that justice is instinct and innate; that the moral sense is as much a part of our constitution as that of feeling, seeing, or hearing, as a wise Creator must have seen to be necessary in an animal destined to live in society; that every human mind feels pleasure in doing good to another. The essence of virtue is in doing good to others, while what is good may be one thing in one society, and its contrary in another.

What more sublime delight than to mingle tears with one whom the hand of heaven hath smitten! To watch over the bed of sickness, and to beguile its tedious and its painful moments! To share our bread with one whom misfortune has let none! This world abounds indeed with misery; to lighten its burden, we must divide it with one another.

I deem it the duty of every man to devote a certain portion of his income for charitable purposes; and that it is his further duty to see it so applied as to do the most good of which it is capable. Take more pleasure in giving what is best to another than in having it for yourself, and then all the world will love you. We should all be of one sect, doers of good, eschewers of evil.

A nation, by establishing a character of liberality and magnanimity, gains in the friendship and respect of others more than the worth of mere money. My public proceedings were always directed by a single view to the best interests of our country. I had no motive to public service but the public satisfaction. I preferred public benefit to all personal considerations and retired much poorer than when I entered the public service. If, in the course of my life, it has been in any degree useful to the cause of humanity, the fact itself bears its full reward.

I came of age in 1764, and was soon put into the nomination of justice of the county in which I lived, and, at the first election following, I became one of the representatives in the Virginia Legislature. I was thence sent to the old Congress. Then employed two years with Mr. Pendleton and Mr. Wythe, on the revisal and reduction to a single code of the whole body of the British Statutes, the acts of our Assembly, and certain parts of the common law. Then elected Governor. Next, to the Legislature, and to Congress again. Sent to Europe as Minister Plenipotentiary. Appointed Secretary of State to the new Government of the United States. Elected Vice-President, and President. And lastly, a Visitor and Rector of the University of Virginia. In these different offices, with scarcely any interval between them, I have been in the public service now sixty-one years; and during the far greater part of the time, in foreign countries or in other States.

I have done for my country, and for all mankind, all that I could do, and I now resign my soul, without fear, to my God; my daughter, to my country.

FORGIVENESS

... Burn Our Old Accounts ...

In little disputes with your companions, give way rather than insist on trifles, for their love and the approbation of others will be worth more to you than the trifle in dispute. Try to let everybody's faults be forgotten, as you would wish yours to be. It is useless to discuss old bankrupt scores. We will therefore burn our old accounts.

Harmony in the married state is the very first object to be aimed at. Nothing can preserve affections uninterrupted but a firm resolution never to differ in will, and a determination in each to consider the love of the other as of more value than any object whatever on which a wish had been fixed. How light, in fact, is the sacrifice of any other wish when weighed against the affections of one with whom we are to pass our whole life! And though opposition in a single instance will hardly of itself produce alienation, yet everyone has their pouch into which all these little oppositions are put; while that is filling the alienation is insensibly going on, and when filled it is complete.

In stating prudential rules for our government in society, I must not omit the important one of never entering into a dispute or argument with another. I never saw an instance of one of two disputants convincing the other by argument. I have seen many, on their getting warm, becoming rude, and shooting one another. Conviction is the effect of our own dispassionate reasoning, either in solitude, or weighing within ourselves, dispassionately, what we hear from others, standing uncommitted in argument ourselves. It was one of the rules which, above all others, made Dr. Franklin the most amiable of men in society, "never to contradict anybody." If he was urged to announce an opinion, he did it rather by asking questions, as if for information, or by suggesting doubts.

When I hear another express an opinion which is not mine, I say to myself, he has a right to his opinion, as I to mine; why should I question it? His error does me no injury, and shall I become a Don Quixote, to bring all men by force of argument to one opinion? If a fact be misstated, it is probable he is gratified by a belief of it, and I have no right to deprive him of the gratification. If he wants information, he will ask for it, and then I will give it in measured terms; but if he still believes his own story, and shows a desire to dispute the fact with me, I hear him and say nothing. It is his affair, not mine, if he prefers error. I tolerate with the utmost latitude the right of others to differ from me in opinion without imputing to them criminality. I know too well the weakness and uncertainty of human reason to wonder at its different results.

Cruel and sanguinary laws defeat their own purpose, by engaging the benevolence of mankind to withhold prosecutions, to smother testimony, or to listen to it with bias, when, if the punishment were only proportioned to the injury, men would feel it their inclination, as well as their duty, to see the laws observed. It may be mentioned as a proof, both the lenity of our government, and the unanimity of its inhabitants, that though the Revolutionary War has now raged near seven years, not a single execution for treason has taken place. Treasons, taking the simulated with the real, are sufficiently punished by exile.

I shall often go wrong through defect of judgment. When right, I shall often be thought wrong by those whose positions will not command a view of the whole ground. I ask your indulgence for my errors, which will never be intentional; and your support against the errors of others, who may condemn what they would not if seen in all its parts. The approbation implied by your suffrage is a consolation to me for the past; and my future solicitude will be to retain the good opinion of those who have bestowed it in advance, to conciliate that of others by doing them all the good in my power, and to be instrumental to the happiness and freedom of all.

It is an unpleasant circumstance, if I am destined to stay here, that the great proportion of those of the place who figure are Federalists, and most of them of the violent kind. Some have been so personally bitter that they can never forgive me, though I do them with sincerity. Perhaps in time they will get tamed. If we can but avoid shocking their feelings by unnecessary acts of severity against their late friends, they will in a little time cement and form one mass with us, and by these means harmony and union be restored to our country, which would be the greatest good we could effect. It was a conviction that these people did not differ from us in principle, which induced me to define the principles which I deemed orthodox, and to urge a reunion on these principles; and I am induced to hope it has conciliated many.

There are no mysteries in the public administration. Difficulties indeed sometimes arise; but common sense and honest intentions will generally steer through them, and, where they cannot be surmounted, I have ever seen the well-intentioned part of our fellow citizens sufficiently disposed not to look for impossibilities. We all know that a farm, however large, is not more difficult to direct than a garden, and does not call for more attention or skill.

I cannot have escaped error. It is incident to our imperfect nature. But I may say with truth, my errors have been of the understanding, not of intention; and that the advancement of the people's rights and interests has been the constant motive of every measure. For honest errors, indulgence may be hoped.

LOVE

... Effusions of the Heart ...

I feel extraordinary gratification in addressing this letter to you, with whom shades of difference in political sentiment have not prevented the interchange of good opinion, nor cut off the friendly offices of society and good correspondence. This political tolerance is the more valued by me, who considers social harmony as the first of human felicities, and the happiest moments, those which are given to the effusions of the heart.

It has been a source of great pain to me, to have met with so many among our opponents, who had not the liberality to distinguish between political and social opposition; who transferred at once to the person, the hatred they bore to his political opinions. I hope that time, the assuager of all evils, will heal these also. One side fears most the ignorance of the people; the other, the selfishness of rulers independent of them. Which is right, time and experience will prove. My anxieties on this subject will never carry me beyond the use of fair and honorable means, of truth and reason; nor have they ever lessened my esteem for moral worth, nor alienated my affections from a single friend, who did not first withdraw himself.

Your principles and dispositions were made to be honored, revered, and loved. True to a single object, the freedom and happiness of man, they have not veered about with the changelings and apostates of our acquaintance. May heaven favor your cause, and make you the channel through which it may pour its favors.

I am happy to find that you are on good terms with your neighbors. It is almost the most important circumstance in life, since nothing is so corroding as frequently to meet persons with whom one has any difference. The ill-will of a single neighbor is an immense drawback on the happiness of life, and therefore their goodwill cannot be bought too dear.

Let us come together as friends and explain to each other what is misrepresented or misunderstood, the clouds will fly away like morning fog, and the sun of friendship appear and shine forever bright and clear. Friendship is precious, not only in the shade, but in the sunshine of life; and thanks to a benevolent arrangement of things, the greater part of life is sunshine.

An honest heart being the first blessing, a knowing head is the second. Lose no moment in improving your head, nor any opportunity of exercising your heart in benevolence. Be you the link of love, union, and peace for the whole family. The world will give you the more credit for it, in proportion to the difficulty of the task, and your own happiness will be the greater as you perceive that you promote that of others.

My hand denies itself farther, every letter admonishing me, by a pain, that it is time to finish, but my heart would go on in expressing to you all its friendship. The happiest moments it knows are those in which it is pouring forth its affections to a few esteemed characters. Friendship is like wine, raw when new, ripened with age, the true old man's milk and restorative cordial. I find as I grow older, that I love those most whom I loved first.

The friendship which has subsisted between us, now half a century, and the harmony of our political principles and pursuits, have been sources of constant happiness to me through that long period. And if I remove beyond the bourne of life itself, as I soon must, it is a comfort to leave the University under your care, and an assurance that it will not be wanting. It has also been a great solace to me, to believe that you are engaged in vindicating to posterity the course we have pursued for preserving to them, in all their purity, the blessings of self-government, which we had assisted too in acquiring for them. If ever the earth has beheld a system of administration conducted with a single and steadfast eye to the general interest and happiness of those committed to it, one which, protected by truth, can never know reproach, it is that to which our lives have been devoted. To myself you have been a pillar of support through life. Take care of me when dead, and be assured that I shall leave with you my last affections.

I am sure that I really know many, many things, and none more surely than that I love you with all my heart, and pray for the continuance of your life until you shall be tired of it yourself. If to the dead it is permitted to care for the things of this world, every action of your life will be under my regard.

PATIENCE

... Wait for a Softer Moment ...

Let no proof be too much for either your patience or acquiescence. Much better, if our companion views a thing in a light different from what we do, to leave him in quiet possession of his view. What is the use of rectifying him if the thing be unimportant; and if important, let it pass for the present, and wait for a softer moment and more conciliatory occasion of revising the subject together. Go on then in suffering nothing to ruffle your temper or interrupt that good humor which it is so easy and so important to render habitual.

In truth, politeness is artificial good humor; it covers the natural wants of it, and ends by rendering habitual a substitute nearly equivalent to the real virtue. It is the practice of sacrificing to those whom we meet in society, all the little conveniences and preferences which will gratify them, and deprive us of nothing worth a moment's consideration; it is the giving a pleasing and flattering turn to our expressions, which will conciliate others, and make them pleased with us as well as themselves. How cheap a price for the good will of another!

Take things always by their smooth handle. Never be angry with anybody, nor speak harm of them. Anger only serves to torment ourselves, to divert others, and alienate their esteem. When angry, count ten before you speak; if very angry, an hundred.

Setting aside the ravings of pepper-pot politicians, of whom there are enough in every age and country, I believe it will place us high in the scale of wisdom, to have preserved our country tranquil and prosperous during a contest which prostrated the honor, power, independence, laws, and property of every country on the other side of the Atlantic. Acquiescence under wrong, to a certain degree, is wisdom, and not pusillanimity; and peace and happiness are preferable to that false honor which, by eternal wars, keeps the European people in eternal labor, want, and wretchedness.

I feared from the beginning, that people not yet sufficiently enlightened for self government, after wading through blood and slaughter, would end in military tyrannies, more or less numerous. Yet as they wished to try the experiment, I wished them success in it. More than a generation will be requisite, under the administration of reasonable laws favoring the progress of knowledge in the general mass of the people, and their habituation to an independent security of person and property, before they will be capable of estimating the value of freedom, and the necessity of a sacred adherence to the principles on which it rests for preservation. Instead of that liberty which takes root and growth in the progress of reason, if recovered by mere force or accident it becomes, with an unprepared people, a tyranny still, of the many, the few, or the one.

A little patience, and we shall see the reign of witches pass over, their spells dissolve, and the people, recovering their true sight, restore their government to its true principles. We must have longer endurance then with our brethren while under delusion; give them time for reflection and experience of consequences; and keep ourselves in a situation to profit by the chapter of accidents. Patience will bring all to rights, and steady perseverance on our part will secure the blessed end.

Self-Discipline

... Find Means Within Ourselves ...

Whenever you feel a warmth of temper rising check it at once, and suppress it, recollecting it will make you unhappy within yourself and disliked by others. Nothing gives one person so great an advantage over another as to remain always cool and unruffled under all circumstances. The prudence and temperance of your discussions will promote that conciliation which so much befriends rational conclusion.

Strive to be good under every situation and to all living creatures. Never trouble another for what you can do yourself. Remote from all other aid, we are obliged to invent and to execute; to find means within ourselves, and not to lean on others. Dependence begets subservience and venality, suffocates the germ of virtue, and prepares fit tools for the designs of ambition.

Take any race of animals, confine them in idleness, whether in a stye, a stable, or a state-room, pamper them with high diet, gratify all their sexual appetites, immerse them in sensualities, nourish their passions, let everything bend before them, and banish whatever might lead them to think, and in a few generations they become all body and no mind. In a world which furnishes so many employments which are so useful, so many which are amusing, it is our own fault if we ever know what ennui is, or if we are driven to the miserable resource of gaming, which corrupts our dispositions and teaches us a habit of hostility against all mankind.

Never buy what you do not want, because it is cheap; it will be dear to you. Never spend your money before you have it. We shall all consider ourselves unauthorized to saddle posterity with our debts, and morally bound to pay them ourselves; and consequently within what may be deemed the period of a generation, or the life of the majority. Having seen the people of all other nations bowed down to the earth under the wars and prodigalities of their rulers, I have cherished their opposites, peace, economy, and riddance of public debt, believing that these are the high road to public as well as to private prosperity and happiness.

If there be one principle more deeply rooted than any other in the mind of every American, it is, that we should have nothing to do with conquest. The energies of the nation, as depends on me, shall be reserved for improvement of the condition of man, not wasted in his destruction. The lamentable resource of war is not authorized for evils of imagination, but for those actual injuries only, which would be more destructive of our well-being than war itself. Peace, justice, and liberal intercourse with all the nations of the world, will, I hope, with all nations, characterize this commonwealth. Friendly nations always negotiate little differences in private. I hope our wisdom will grow with our power, and teach us, that the less we use our power, the greater it will be.

I was a hard student until I entered on the business of life, the duties of which leave no idle time to those disposed to fulfill them; and now, retired, I am again a hard student. Our projected college, the University of Virginia, gives me constant employment; for, being the only visitor in its immediate neighborhood, all its administrative business falls on me, and that, while building is going on, is not a little.

We studiously avoid too much government at the college. We treat the students as men and gentlemen, under the guidance mainly of their own discretion. They so consider themselves, and make it their pride to acquire that character for their institution. We have spent the prime of our lives in procuring them the precious blessing of liberty. Let them spend theirs in showing that it is the great parent of science and of virtue; and that a nation will be great in both, always in proportion as it is free.

NOT FEARING LOSS

... The Evils Which Have Never Happened ...

To procure tranquility of mind we must avoid desire and fear, the two principal diseases of the mind. Man is a free agent. Virtue consists in, 1. Prudence. 2. Temperance. 3. Fortitude. 4. Justice. To which are opposed, 1. Folly. 2. Desire. 3. Fear. 4. Deceit. Never throw off the best affections of nature in the moment when they become most precious to their object; nor fear to extend your hand to save another, less you should sink yourself.

Never fear the want of business. A man who qualifies himself well for his calling, never fails of employment in it. I am not myself apt to be alarmed at innovations recommended by reason. That dread belongs to those whose interests or prejudices shrink from the advance of truth and science. Here, where all is new, no innovation is feared which offers good.

I am not among those who fear the people. They, and not the rich, are our dependence for continued freedom. The cherishment of the people is our principle, the fear and distrust of them, that of the other party. It is not inclination in any body, but a fear of the opinion of the world which leads men to the absurd and immoral decision of differences by duel.

Let those flatter who fear; it is not an American art. I never had an opinion in politics or religion which I was afraid to own. I fear no injury which any man can do me. I have never done a single act, or been concerned in any transaction, which I fear to have fully laid open, or which could do me any hurt if truly stated. I have never done a single thing with a view to my personal interest, or that of any friend, or with any other view than that of the greatest public good; therefore, no threat or fear on that head will ever be a motive of action with me.

As to federal slanders, I never wished them to be answered, but by the tenor of my life, half a century of which has been on a theater at which the public have been spectators, and competent judges of its merit. Their approbation has taught a lesson, useful to the world, that the man who fears no truths has nothing to fear from lies. I should have fancied myself half guilty had I condescended to put pen to paper in refutation of their falsehoods, or drawn to them respect by any notice from myself.

You ask, if I would agree to live my seventy or rather seventy-three years over again? To which I say yes. I think with you, that it is a good world on the whole; that it has been framed on a principle of benevolence, and more pleasure than pain dealt out to us. There are, indeed, (who might say nay) gloomy and hypochondriac minds, inhabitants of diseased bodies, disgusted with the present, and despairing of the future; always counting that the worst will happen, because it may happen. To these I say, how much pain have cost us the evils which have never happened! My temperament is sanguine. I steer my bark with Hope in the head, leaving Fear in the stern.

SILENCE

... A Noiseless Course ...

Wars and contentions, indeed, fill the pages of history with more matter. But more blessed is that nation whose silent course of happiness furnishes nothing for history to say. This is what I ambition for my own country.

From a very early period of my life, I laid it down as a rule of conduct, never to write a word for the public papers. From this, I have never departed in a single instance. In the election of 1800, I held no councils with anybody respecting it, nor suffered any one to speak to me on the subject, believing it my duty to leave myself to the free discussion of the public.

I shall pursue in silence the path of right. The path we have to pursue is so quiet that we have nothing scarcely to propose to our Legislature. A noiseless course, not meddling with the affairs of others, unattractive of notice, is a mark that society is going on in happiness. The less that is said about any constitutional difficulty, the better; and that it will be desirable for Congress to do what is necessary, in silence.

I confess that I am not reconciled to the idea of a chief magistrate parading himself through the several States, as an object of public gaze, and in quest of an applause which, to be valuable, should be purely voluntary. I had rather acquire silent goodwill by a faithful discharge of my duties, than owe expressions of it to my putting myself in the way of receiving them. I am sincerely mortified to be thus brought forward on the public stage, where to remain, to advance, or to retire, will be equally against my love of silence and quiet, and my abhorrence of dispute. My great wish is to go on in a strict but silent performance of my duty.

Long tried in the school of affliction, no loss which can rend the human heart is unknown to mine; and a like one particularly, at about the same period of life, had taught me to feel the sympathies of yours. The same experience has proved that time, silence, and occupation are its only medicines.

Be a listener only, keep within yourself, and endeavor to establish within yourself a habit of silence. I think one travels more usefully when alone, because he reflects more. To every obstacle, oppose patience, perseverance, and soothing language. A firm, but quiet opposition will be the most likely to succeed. We often repent of what we have said, but never of that which we have not.

Say nothing of my religion. It is known to my God and myself alone. Its evidence before the world is to be sought in my life; if that has been honest and dutiful to society, the religion which has regulated it cannot be a bad one. Religion is not the subject for you and me; neither of us know the religious opinions of the other; that is a matter between our Maker and ourselves. I have left the world, in silence, to judge of causes from their effects.

Truth Seeking

... Enlighten the People Generally ...

Be industrious in advancing yourself in knowledge, which with your good dispositions, will ensure the love of others, and your own happiness. A patient pursuit of facts, and cautious combination and comparison of them, is the drudgery to which man is subjected by his Maker, if he wishes to attain sure knowledge. I am myself an empiric in natural philosophy, suffering my faith to go no further than my facts. I am satisfied, and sufficiently occupied with the things which are, without tormenting or troubling myself about those which may indeed be, but of which I have no evidence.

Follow truth as the only safe guide, and eschew error, which bewilders us in one false consequence after another, in endless succession. He who knows nothing is nearer the truth than he whose mind is filled with falsehoods and errors. It is always better to have no ideas than false ones; to believe nothing than to believe what is wrong. No vice is so mean as the want of truth, and at the same time so useless. Truth is the first object.

Your reason is now mature enough to examine the object of religion. In the first place, divest yourself of all bias in favor of novelty and singularity of opinion. Indulge them in any other subject rather than that of religion. It is too important, and the consequences of error may be too serious. On the other hand, shake off all the fears and servile prejudices, under which weak minds are servilely crouched. Fix reason firmly in her seat, and call to her tribunal every fact, every opinion. Question with boldness even the existence of a God; because, if there be one, he must more approve of the homage of reason, than that of blindfolded fear.

Almighty God hath created the mind free, and manifested His supreme will that free it shall remain by making it altogether insusceptible of restraint. All attempts to influence it by temporal punishments or burthens, or by civil incapacitations, tend only to beget habits of hypocrisy and meanness, and are a departure from the plan of the Holy Author of our religion, who, being Lord both of body and mind, yet chose not to propagate it by coercions on either, as was in his Almighty power to do, but to exalt it by its influence on reason alone.

The most effectual means of preventing the perversion of power into tyranny are to illuminate, as far as practicable, the minds of the people. It is an insult to our citizens to question whether they are rational beings or not, and blasphemy against religion to suppose it cannot stand the test of truth and reason. Light and liberty go together. I look to the diffusion of light and education as the resource most to be relied on for ameliorating the condition, promoting the virtue, and advancing the happiness of man. Enlighten the people generally, and tyranny and oppressions of body and mind will vanish like evil spirits at the dawn of day. If a nation expects to be ignorant and free, in a state of civilization, it expects what never was and never will be. No nation is permitted to live in ignorance with impunity.

Truth advances, and error recedes step by step only; and to do our fellow-men the most good in our power, we must lead where we can, follow where we cannot, and still go with them, watching always the favorable moment for helping them to another step. Truth will do well enough if left to shift for herself. She seldom has received much aid from the power of great men to whom she is rarely known and seldom welcome. She has no need of force to procure entrance into the minds of men.

Truth is the proper and sufficient antagonist to error, and has nothing to fear from the conflict, unless by human interposition disarmed of her natural weapons, free argument and debate; errors ceasing to be dangerous when it is permitted freely to contradict them. Truth and reason are eternal. They have prevailed. And they will eternally prevail.

PEACE PRAYER

... Run the Race of Peace ...

Peace is our passion. I have ever cherished the same spirit with all nations, from a consciousness that peace, prosperity, liberty, and morals, have an intimate connection. From the moment which sealed our peace and independence, our nation has wisely pursued the paths of peace and justice. Peace and justice should be the polar stars of the American societies.

The happiness of mankind is best promoted by the useful pursuits of peace. Our desire is to pursue ourselves the path of peace as the only one leading surely to prosperity. Go on in doing with your pen what in other times was done with the sword; show that reformation is more practicable by operation on the mind than on the body of man. Peace and friendship with all mankind is our wisest policy.

I believe that through all America there has been but a single sentiment on the subject of peace and war, which was in favor of the former. I abhor war and view it as the greatest scourge of mankind. I love peace, and am anxious that we should give the world still another useful lesson, by showing them other modes of punishing than by war, which is as much a punishment to the punisher as to the sufferer. If nations go to war for every degree of injury, there would never be peace on earth. We think that peaceable means may be devised of keeping nations in the path of justice towards us, by making justice their interest, and injuries to react on themselves. We have, therefore, remained in peace, suffering frequent injuries, but, on the whole, multiplying, improving, prospering beyond all example. Peace has been our principle, peace is our interest, and peace has saved to the world this only plant of free and rational government now existing in it. My hope is in peace.

Thanks be to God that Napoleon, the tiger who reveled so long in the blood and spoils of Europe is at length, like another Prometheus, chained to his rock, where the vulture of remorse for his crimes will be preying on his vitals and in like manner without consuming them. Having been, like him, intrusted with the happiness of my country, I feel the blessing of resembling him in no other point. I have not caused the death of five or ten millions of human beings, the devastation of other countries, the depopulation of my own, the exhaustion of all its resources, the destruction of its liberties, nor its foreign subjugation. All this he has done to render more illustrious the atrocities perpetrated for illustrating himself and his family with plundered diadems and sceptres. On the contrary, I have the consolation to reflect that during the period of my administration not a drop of blood of a single fellow citizen was shed by the sword of war or of the law, and that after cherishing for eight years their peace and prosperity I laid down their trust of my own accord and in the midst of their blessings and importunities to continue in it.

It will be a true testimony of my principles and persuasion that the state of peace is that which most improves the manners and morals, the prosperity and happiness of mankind; and although I dare not promise myself that it can be perpetually maintained, yet if, by the inculcations of reason or religion, the perversities of our nature can be so far corrected as sometimes to prevent the necessity, either supposed or real, of an appeal to the blinder scourges of war, murder, and devastation, the benevolent endeavors of the friends of peace will not be entirely without remuneration. I hope we shall prove how much happier for man the Quaker policy is, and that the life of the feeder, is better than that of the fighter.

I wish that all nations may recover and retain their independence; that those which are overgrown may not advance beyond safe measures of power, that a salutary balance may be ever maintained among nations, and that our peace, commerce, and friendship, may be sought and cultivated by all. My hope of preserving peace for our country is not founded in the greater principles of non-resistance under every wrong, but in the belief that a just and friendly conduct on our part will produce justice and friendship from others.

We, I hope, shall be permitted to run the race of peace. To preserve and secure peace has been the constant aim of my administration. Twenty years of peace, and the prosperity so visibly flowing from it, have but strengthened our attachment to it, and the blessings it brings, and we do not despair of being always a peaceable nation. I pray for peace, as best for all the world, best for us, and best for me, who have already lived to see three wars. That peace, safety, and concord may be long enjoyed by our fellow-citizens is the most ardent wish of my heart, and if I can be instrumental in procuring or preserving them, I shall think I have not lived in vain.

Heaven bless you, and guard you under all circumstances; give you smooth waters, gentle breezes, and clear skies, hushing all its elements into peace.

Lord, now lettest thou thy servant depart in peace.

LIGHT AND LIBERTY

"Light and liberty go together."

—THOMAS JEFFERSON TO TENCH COXE, 1795

CHRONOLOGY

1743   Born April 13 in Virginia at Shadwell, near Charlottesville, the son of Peter Jefferson and Jane Randolph.

1757   Father dies.

1758   Attends Reverend Maury's school.

1760   Enters the College of William and Mary.

1762   Graduates college and begins law studies under George Wythe at William and Mary.

1767   Commences seven-year legal practice.

1769   Elected to the Virginia House of Burgesses, serving until 1775.

1769   Begins building Monticello from his own architectural design.

1772   Marries Martha Wayles Skelton.

1773   Key organizer of Committees of Correspondence with other colonies.

1774   Writes "A Summary View of the Rights of British America."

1775   Elected Virginia delegate to the Continental Congress in Philadelphia.

1776 Writes the Declaration of Independence.

1776 Elected Albemarle County Representative in the Virginia House of Delegates.

1776 Drafts a proposed constitution for Virginia.

1779 Completes proposed revision of a substantial portion of Virginia's statutes.

1779 Elected wartime Governor of Virginia and after reelection serves two years.

1782 Wife, Martha, dies having borne six children, two of whom survive infancy.

1782 Writes substantial portions of his only book, *Notes on the State of Virginia*.

1783 Serves as a Virginia delegate in Congress.

1784 Drafts "Report on Government for Western Territory."

1784 Sent by Congress to Paris to negotiate commercial treaties.

1785 Appointed Minister to France, succeeding Benjamin Franklin.

1786 Virginia enacts Jefferson's "Statute for Religious Freedom."

1787 Tours southern France and northern Italy.

1788 Tours the Netherlands and the Rhineland.

1789 Witnesses the opening events of the French Revolution.

1790 Appointed Secretary of State by George Washington.

1794 Returns to farming and rebuilds Monticello.

1796 Elected Vice President of the United States under John Adams.

1797 Elected President of the American Philosophical Society, serving until 1814.

1798 Drafts Kentucky resolutions declaring unconstitutional the federalists' Alien and Sedition acts.

1801 Elected third President of the United States.

1803 Concludes Louisiana Purchase and mounts the "voyage of discovery" of the new land under Meriwether Lewis.

1805 Reelected President.

1806   Begins construction of second home at Poplar Forest, Bedford County, Virginia.

1807   Implements Embargo Act, seeking to use economic coersion to avoid war with Great Britain.

1808   Declines a third term as President.

1809   Retires to Monticello.

1815   Sells his library to the United States, forming the foundation of the Library of Congress.

1819   Founds the University of Virginia.

1819   Completes "The Life and Morals of Jesus of Nazareth" for personal use.

1820   Protests the Missouri Compromise.

1821   Writes "Autobiography" for his family.

1823   Advocates the policy underlying the Monroe Doctrine.

1825   University of Virginia admits first students.

1826   Dies on July 4 at Monticello.

NOTES

The only roughly complete sources of the entirety of Thomas Jefferson's writings remain *The Writings of Thomas Jefferson* (10 vols., Paul Leicester Ford, ed., New York, 1892–99), the more accurate collection, and *The Writings of Thomas Jefferson* (20 vols., Andrew A. Lipscomb and Albert Ellery Bergh, eds., Washington, 1903–04), which is more complete. Most of the quotations that comprise this book were drawn from the Lipscomb and Bergh edition. Lipscomb and Bergh built on two earlier nineteenth-century collections: *Memoirs, Correspondence and Miscellany from the Papers of Thomas Jefferson* (4 vols., Thomas Jefferson Randolph, ed., Charlottesville, 1829) and *The Writings of Thomas Jefferson* (9 vols., Henry A. Washington, ed., New York, 1853–54). *The Jeffersonian Cyclopedia* (New York, 1900), a remarkable volume in which John P. Foley compiled and organized alphabetically under nine thousand titles short Jefferson observations on a wide array of topics, was also a useful source.

Thomas Jefferson, Writings (Merrill D. Peterson, ed., New York, 1984) is the most comprehensive single volume of the works of Thomas Jefferson. The definitive modern edition of Thomas Jefferson's writings, *The Papers of Thomas Jefferson*, is in the hands of Princeton University. Thirty volumes covering Jefferson's life through the late 1790s have been published since the endeavor began in 1943. Responsibility for Jefferson's papers following his retirement from the Presidency in 1809 has been assumed recently by the Thomas Jefferson Foundation. Their concurrent efforts should accelerate the completion of this monumental task.

FAITH

I have ever . . . must judge me: TJ to Mrs. M. Harrison Smith, August 6, 1816.

Hitherto I have . . . us always unerring: TJ to Miles King, September 26, 1814.

Faith and works . . . before God's tribunal: TJ to Charles Thomson, January 29, 1817.

If no action . . . see into them: TJ to Martin Van Buren, June 29, 1824.

There is only . . . sum of religion: TJ to Benjamin Waterhouse, June 26, 1822.

I hold (without . . . and other forms: TJ to John Adams, April 11, 1823.

When great evils . . . producing some good: TJ to Dr. Benjamin Rush, September 23, 1800.

We are not . . . His own time: TJ to David Barrow, May 1, 1815.

Our next meeting . . . is essentially benevolent: TJ to Abigail Adams, January 11, 1817.

Adore God; reverence . . . and ineffable bliss: TJ to Thomas Jefferson Smith, February 21, 1825.

HAPPINESS

Be assiduous in . . . are easily obtained: TJ to Peter Carr, May 28, 1788.

Happiness is the . . . test of virtue: TJ to William Short, October 31, 1819.

If the wise . . . happiness cannot be: TJ to Amos J. Cook, January 21, 1816.

Interesting occupations are . . . of finding employment: TJ to Martha Jefferson Randolph, April 26, 1791.

A mind always . . . the only wretched: TJ to Martha Jefferson, May 21, 1787.

The Giver of . . . not for wretchedness: TJ to James Monroe, May 20, 1782.

All men are . . . pursuit of happiness: Declaration of Independence as Drawn by Jefferson, 1776.

Perfect happiness, I . . . have steadfastly believed: TJ to John Page, July 15, 1763.

Nothing makes me . . . of whatever description: TJ to Samuel Osgood, October 5, 1785.

There are minds . . . are to it: TJ to Alexander Donald, February 7, 1788.

Honesty, disinterestedness, and . . . our happiness depends: TJ to Francis Eppes, May 21, 1816.

Entertaining a due . . . and happy people?: First Inaugural Address, March 4, 1801.

A constitution has . . . has ever shone: TJ to John Adams, October 28, 1813.

The only orthodox . . . associated under it: TJ to F. A. Van der Kamp, March 22, 1812.

How soon the . . . nobles, and priests: TJ to Ellen W. Coolidge, August 27, 1825.

If we can . . . must become happy: TJ to Thomas Cooper, November 29, 1802.

We who have . . . within their choice: TJ to Charles Pinckney, September 30, 1820.

If, in my . . . of good government: TJ to the Republican Citizens of Washington County, Maryland, March 31, 1809.

We wish the . . . of every nation: TJ to Madame Anne Louise Germaine Necker de Staël, July 3, 1815.

It will give . . . hours of society: TJ to José Francisco Correa de Serra, April 19, 1814.

Is it impossible . . . of human nature?: TJ to John Louis de Unger, November 30, 1780.

I am as . . . end, at Monticello: TJ to Dr. George Gilmer, August 11, 1787.

God send you . . . as yours affectionately: TJ to General Henry Dearborn, August 14, 1811.

I sincerely supplicate . . . a happy people: TJ to the Tammany Society or Columbian Order of the City of Washington, March 2, 1809.

The religion you . . . be in happiness: TJ to Maria Cosway, December 27, 1820.

ASPIRATION

Nothing can contribute . . . ever yet hysterical: TJ to Martha Jefferson, March 28, 1787.

I am constantly . . . never see again: TJ to Marquis de Lafayette, April 11, 1787.

Our greatest happiness . . . all just pursuits: Notes on the State of Virginia, 1782.

The precept is . . . which is good: TJ to William Drayton, January 13, 1788.

Nothing is troublesome . . . we do willingly: TJ to Thomas Jefferson Smith, February 21, 1825.

In endeavors to . . . should never despair: TJ to John Quincy Adams, November 1, 1817.

Be not weary . . . never be closed: TJ to Spencer Roane, June 27, 1821.

Become an honest . . . whom we live: TJ to Francis Wayles Eppes, September 9, 1814.

Above all things . . . value on ourselves: TJ to Martha Jefferson, April 7, 1787.

Encourage all your . . . moment of death: TJ to Peter Carr, August 19, 1785.

The relations which . . . study and investigation: Minutes as Rector of the University of Virginia, October 7, 1822.

I never go . . . with the sun: TJ to Dr. Vine Utley, March 21, 1819.

Of those recorded . . . and Epic poetry: TJ to Robert Skipwith, August 3, 1771.

It is part . . . resolution and contrivance: TJ to Martha Jefferson, March 28, 1787.

When we see . . . our own torment: TJ to Mary Jefferson, January 7, 1798.

Fortitude teaches us . . . of our road: TJ to William Short, June 22, 1819.

Go on therefore . . . easier and easier: TJ to Thomas Jefferson Randolph, November 24, 1808.

I most cordially . . . thought of retiring: TJ to Dr. James Currie, August 4, 1787.

You tell me . . . and lean together?: TJ to John Adams, January 8, 1825.

FITNESS

Without health there . . . the wisest valetudinarian: TJ to Thomas Mann Randolph, July 6, 1787.

Knowledge indeed is . . . is more so: TJ to Thomas Mann Randolph, August 27, 1786.

In my view . . . functions and actions: TJ to Dr. Thomas Cooper, October 7, 1814.

Take a great . . . and on foot: TJ to Peter Carr, August 10, 1787.

Of all exercises . . . or long lived: TJ to Thomas Mann Randolph, August 27, 1786.

Love of repose . . . things from happiness: TJ to William Short, October 19, 1819.

Never think of . . . objects surrounding you: TJ to Peter Carr, August 19, 1785.

A little walk . . . to the mind: Ibid.

The weather should . . . every other description: TJ to Thomas Mann Randolph, August 27, 1786.

The sun is my almighty physician: TJ to James Monroe, March 18, 1785.

Having been so . . . as human life: TJ to Dr. Casper Wistar, June 21, 1807.

I have lived . . . in any form: TJ to Dr. Vine Utley, March 21, 1819.

I have for . . . to that practice: TJ to James Maury, June 16, 1815.

I enjoy good . . . thirty or forty: TJ to Dr. Vine Utley, March 21, 1819.

The loss of . . . after my affairs: TJ to Dr. Benjamin Rush, August 17, 1811.

The sovereign invigorator of the body is exercise: TJ to Thomas Mann Randolph, August 27, 1786.

CHEERFULNESS

Exercise and application . . . to our friends: TJ to Martha Jefferson, March 28, 1787.

Husband well your . . . everybody your friend: TJ to Peter Carr, August 19, 1785.

All the world . . . well as reflection: TJ to Mary Jefferson, June 14, 1797.

Life is of . . . and promotes health: TJ to James Madison, February 20, 1784.

I estimate the . . . rigorist in morality: TJ to Dr. Benjamin Rush, January 3, 1808.

Good humor is . . . first rate value: TJ to Thomas Jefferson Randolph, November 24, 1808.

Nothing enables a . . . a smooth temper: Notes on a Conversation with Erskine, November 9, 1808.

I have been . . . impression on me: TJ to General James Wilkinson, March 10, 1811.

Though I have . . . of their teeth: TJ to Samuel Smith, August 22, 1798.

I do not . . . in its favor: TJ to John Adams, August 1, 1816.

It is a . . . in some other: TJ to Sir John Sinclair, August 24, 1791.

No man has . . . can, they will: TJ to James Monroe, October 16, 1814.

I cannot act . . . honesty of man: TJ to Thomas Leiper, January 1, 1814.

Our administration now . . . of the nation: TJ to Albert Gallatin, October 12, 1806.

That others may . . . our personal knowledge: TJ to Abner Watkins and Bernard Todd, December 21, 1807.

Our ship is . . . my daily prayers: TJ to John Melish, March 10, 1811.

Contemplating the union . . . of his fathers: Second Inaugural Address, March 4, 1805.

I yield the . . . succeed to them: TJ to General James Breckenridge, February 15, 1821.

I pray you . . . more confidently count: TJ to Marquis de Lafayette, June 19, 1796.

Should it be . . . it with cheerfulness: TJ to John Adams, November 19, 1785.

GRATITUDE

Called upon to . . . so justly inspire: First Inaugural Address, March 4, 1801.

When we assemble . . . for His bounty: Second Annual Message to Congress, December 15, 1802.

Among the most . . . is best support: TJ to Captain John Thomas, November 18, 1807.

I have but . . . promotes their happiness: TJ to Madame la Duchess D'Auville, April 2, 1790.

While we devoutly . . . has been preserved: First Annual Message to Congress, December 8, 1801.

Among the felicities . . . worthy of it: TJ to Isaac Weaver, June 7, 1807.

It is wise . . . we have not: TJ to Abigail Adams, January 11, 1817.

Lose no occasion . . . increase your worth: TJ to Peter Carr, August 10, 1787.

Everything is useful . . . grateful acts also: TJ to Robert Skipwith, August 3, 1771.

I thank you . . . animate my breast: TJ to the Democratic Citizens of Adams County, Pennsylvania, March 20, 1808.

SINCERITY

I am made . . . honestly and conscientiously: TJ to Dr. Benjamin Rush, March 24, 1801.

I would be . . . my duty, alert: TJ to James Madison, December 20, 1787.

Should my views . . . suggestion of them: TJ to James Madison, May 21, 1813.

I know but . . . in the latter: TJ to James Madison, August 28, 1789.

Honesty is the . . . Book of Wisdom: TJ to Nathaniel Macon, January 12, 1819.

Let it be . . . a just nation: Third Annual Message to Congress, October 17, 1803.

The exact truth should be told: TJ to Joseph Coolidge, October 13, 1825.

They will believe . . . the bad also: TJ to James Monroe, January 1, 1815.

Honesty promotes interest in the long run: TJ to Thomas Law, June 13, 1814.

I can conscientiously . . . should be unknown: TJ to James Main, October 19, 1808.

The succession to . . . only his successor": TJ to Reverend William Smith, February 19, 1791.

I hope I . . . of our country: TJ to Dr. Elijah Griffith, May 28, 1809.

I meddled in . . . no concealed object: Autobiography, 1821.

I disdained all . . . object was pure: TJ to George Washington, December 31, 1793.

The whole art . . . where you fail: Autobiography, 1821.

Let common sense . . . things to rights: TJ to Dr. Ezra Stiles, December 24, 1786.

I have received . . . have done it: TJ to Nathaniel Macon, November 23, 1821.

Sincerity I value . . . efforts in vain: TJ to William Duane, March 22, 1806.

I disdain everything like duplicity: TJ to James Madison, August 3, 1797.

Good faith is every man's surest guide: Draft for Proclamation Announcing Ratification of Definitive Peace Treaty, January 14, 1784.

Of you, my . . . with conscious security: Address to the Inhabitants of Albemarle County, April 3, 1809.

NOT THIRSTING FOR GAIN

When I first . . . increase of fortune: TJ to Joseph Fay, March 18, 1793.

No man ever . . . offices than myself: Notes on Conversations with Washington, March 1, 1792.

In truth, I . . . can be elsewhere: TJ to John Langdon, January 22, 1797.

I have no . . . in a storm: TJ to Edward Rutledge, December 27, 1796.

Whenever a man . . . in his conduct: TJ to Tench Coxe, May 21, 1799.

I love to . . . by their measures: TJ to Edward Rutledge, December 27, 1796.

I have the . . . they are empty: TJ to Count Dionati, March 29, 1807.

The glow of . . . more than money: TJ to Charles McPherson, February 25, 1773.

It is neither . . . which give happiness: TJ to Mrs. A. J. Marks, July 12, 1788.

Wealth, title, and . . . title, and office: TJ to Maria Cosway, October 12, 1786.

I have not . . . with their riches: TJ to Jeremiah Moor, August 14, 1800.

In the great . . . share to himself: TJ to Dr. Joseph Priestley, June 19, 1802.

Greediness for wealth . . . vices of commerce: TJ to John Adams, May 17, 1818.

The selfish spirit . . . that of gain: TJ to Colonel Larkin Smith, April 25, 1804.

Would a missionary . . . my own heart: TJ to John Page, May 4, 1786.

I have never . . . power over others: TJ to Antoine L. C. Destutt de Tracy, January 26, 1811.

I have seen . . . but splendid torments: TJ to Martha Jefferson Randolph, June 8, 1797.

The little spice . . . than present name: TJ to James Madison, April 27, 1795.

Pride costs us . . . thirst, and cold: TJ to Thomas Jefferson Smith, February 21, 1825.

Never did a . . . of public approbation: TJ to Monsieur Pierre Samuel du Pont de
  Nemours, March 2, 1809.

SEEING THE GOOD

You have formed . . . to the world: TJ to W. T. Franklin, May 7, 1786.

Dr. Franklin was . . . which he lived: TJ to Samuel Smith, August 22, 1798.

and the father of American philosophy: TJ to Jonathan Williams, July 3, 1796.

No one of . . . phenomena of nature: Notes on the State of Virginia, 1782.

His memory will . . . heard or feared: TJ to Jonathan Edwards, July 3, 1796.

Hamilton was indeed . . . of a nation: Explanation of the Three Volumes Bound
  in Marbled Paper, February 4, 1818.

George Mason was . . . made it seasonable: Autobiography, 1821.

His character was . . . estimate of it: TJ to Dabney Carr, Jr., January 19, 1816.

We have supposed . . . to this day: Notes on the State of Virginia, 1782.

No man ever . . . of future times: TJ to John Saunderson, August 31, 1820.

I think I . . . an everlasting remembrance: TJ to Dr. Walter Jones, January 2,
  1814.

I can say . . . most sovereign contempt: TJ to Samuel A. Wells, May 12, 1819.

I knew much . . . word he uttered: TJ to John Adams, June 11, 1812.

He was indeed . . . few ever attained: Biographical Sketch, Sent to Joseph
  Delaplaine, July 26, 1816.

My message to . . . enterprise to him: Biographical Sketch, Sent to Paul Allen,
  April 13, 1813.

Trained in the . . . speak for themselves: Autobiography, 1821.

JESUS

Jesus appeared. His . . . and the throne: TJ to Dr. Benjamin Rush, April 21, 1803
  (Syllabus of an Estimate of the Merit of the Doctrines of Jesus,
  Compared with Those of Others).

We find in . . . not been surpassed: TJ to William Short, August 4, 1820.

The practice of . . . in His discourses: TJ to James Fishback, September 27,
  1809.

I have made . . . have never seen: TJ to Charles Thomson, January 9, 1816.

When we shall . . . have been Christian: TJ to Timothy Pickering, February 27,
  1821.

The mild and . . . and common morality: TJ to Elbridge Gerry, March 29, 1801.

It is a . . . which we schismatize: TJ to James Fishback, September 27, 1809.

Religious animosities I . . . which He preaches: TJ to Dr. Ezra Stiles, June 21, 1819.

As to myself . . . who inculcate them: TJ to Thomas Leiper, January 21, 1809.

I am a . . . claimed any other: TJ to Benjamin Rush, April 21, 1803.

NATURE'S BEAUTY

Lake George is . . . it from monotony: TJ to Martha Jefferson Randolph, May 31, 1791.

The passage of . . . the calm below: Notes on the State of Virginia, 1782.

Heidelberg is on . . . distinctly four syllables: Memorandum on a Tour from Paris, March 3, 1788.

The Natural Bridge . . . is really indescribable!: Notes on the State of Virginia, 1782.

And our own . . . to all nature!: TJ to Maria Cosway, October 12, 1786.

HUMILITY

In America no . . . must be wrong: Answers by Mr. Jefferson, to Questions Addressed to Him by Monsieur Meunier, Author of That Part of the Encyclopédie Méthodique Entitled Economie Politique et Diplomatique, June 22, 1786.

I can further . . . parish in America: TJ to General George Washington, May 2, 1788.

The new government . . . in the people: TJ to James Madison, August 28, 1789.

When brought together . . . out of office: Rules of Governmental Etiquette, November 1803.

The fool has . . . master of himself: Address to the Deputies of the Cherokee Upper Towns, January 9, 1809.

The rights of . . . breaks my leg: Notes on the State of Virginia, 1782.

Is this then . . . cut or stretched?: TJ to Monsieur N. G. Dufief, April 19, 1814.

Having been one . . . allotted to me: Reply to Public Address: To the General Assembly of Virginia, February 16, 1809.

I have been . . . transactions to himself: TJ to Skelton Jones, July 28, 1809.

Your statements of . . . of all America: TJ to Joseph Delaplaine, April 12, 1817.

Disapproving myself of . . . of the kind: TJ to Levi Lincoln, August 30, 1803.

SACRIFICE

A recollection of . . . will now maintain: Reply to Public Address: To the Members of the Baltimore Baptist Association, October 17, 1808.

The supremacy of . . . liberty, and safety: First Inaugural Address, March 4, 1801.

A debt of . . . measured to him: TJ to Edward Rutledge, December 27, 1796.

It is for . . . decision between candidates: TJ to John Adams, December 27, 1785.

In a virtuous . . . great private loss: TJ to Richard Henry Lee, June 17, 1779.

A person who . . . of his life: TJ to Governor James Sullivan, March 3, 1808.

To the sacrifice . . . and even reputation: TJ to Dr. James Currie, January 18, 1786.

I have been . . . tempest, fire, etc.: TJ to Peregrine Fitzhugh, February 23, 1798.

Politics, like religion . . . reformers of error: TJ to James Ogilvie, August 4, 1811.

Possessed of the . . . their sole guarantee: Reply to Public Address: To James Hochie, President of the Ancient Plymouth Society of New London, April 2, 1809.

We owe every . . . property, and peace: The Solemn Declaration and Protest of the Commonwealth of Virginia, on the Principles of the Constitution of the United States, and on the Violations of Them, 1825.

The last hope . . . and every enmity: TJ to Colonel William Duane, March 28, 1811.

If ever there . . . gave us independence: TJ to John W. Eppes, November 6, 1813.

The approbation of . . . who follow us: TJ to John Dickinson, December 19, 1801.

I have ever . . . and good will: TJ to Joseph C. Cabell, January 11, 1825.

BEING TRUE TO YOURSELF

Nature has written . . . them for himself: TJ to Thomas Law, June 13, 1814.

If ever you . . . a wrong act: TJ to Martha Jefferson, December 11, 1783.

Conscience is the . . . doubts and inconsistencies: TJ to George Washington, May 10, 1798.

I am of . . . as I know: TJ to Dr. Ezra Stiles, June 25, 1819.

When I am . . . from my nature: TJ to George Washington, June 19, 1796.

I never submitted . . . there at all: TJ to Francis Hopkinson, March 13, 1789.

From the moment . . . over his slanders: TJ to Uriah McGregory, August 13, 1800.

No reformation can . . . is no repentance: TJ to Maria Cosway, October 12, 1786.

Resort is had . . . is against us: TJ to James Madison, May 21, 1813.

Every man's own . . . be his oracle: TJ to Dr. Benjamin Rush, March 6, 1813.

Be assured that . . . what is right: TJ to Thomas Jefferson Randolph,
    November 24, 1808.

Man, once surrendering . . . becomes a wreck: TJ to James Smith, December 8,
    1822.

Is uniformity attainable? . . . over the earth: Notes on the State of Virginia, 1782.

Force cannot give right: A Summary View of the Rights of British America,
    1774.

Mysticisms constitute the . . . an intelligible proposition: TJ to John Adams,
    August 22, 1813.

It behooves every . . . God and himself: TJ to Dr. Benjamin Rush, April 21, 1803.

I never will . . . freedom of conscience: TJ to Edward Dowse, April 19, 1803.

All this, my . . . decide for yourself: TJ to John Adams, June 27, 1813.

SELF-PERFECTION

Be very select . . . easy and tranquil: TJ to Thomas Jefferson Randolph,
    November 24, 1808.

When I recollect . . . me their approbation?: Ibid.

A determination never . . . of the world: Ibid.

Go on deserving . . . to be industrious: TJ to John Wayles Eppes, July 28, 1787.

Do not be . . . themselves in practice: TJ to John Taylor, November 26, 1798.

Practice in this . . . of insuperable difficulty: TJ to Thomas Jefferson Randolph,
    May 14, 1810.

Experience alone brings skill: TJ to William H. Crawford, February 11, 1815.

It will be . . . in the end: TJ to Gideon Granger, April 16, 1804.

Take from man . . . without a competitor: TJ to Thomas Law, June 13, 1814.

Bold, unequivocal virtue . . . even to ambition: TJ to John Jay, June 17, 1789.

Nature has constituted . . . test of virtue: TJ to Thomas Law, June 13, 1814.

The want or . . . reason and calculation: Ibid.

You may give . . . unworthy of notice: TJ to Gideon Granger, March 9, 1814.

The uniform tenor . . . which do not: TJ to George Clinton, December 31, 1803.

I never did . . . a private man: TJ to Don Valentine de Feronda, October 4, 1809.

There is not . . . the whole world: TJ to Henry Lee, May 15, 1826.

DOING WHAT IS RIGHT

If ever you . . . becomes more exposed: TJ to Peter Carr, August 19, 1785.

Give up money . . . and act accordingly: Ibid.

The precept of . . . issue to Him: TJ to Maria Cosway, October 12, 1786.

It is of . . . its good dispositions: TJ to Peter Carr, August 19, 1785.

Honesty which proceeds . . . surely counted on: TJ to James Madison, June 20, 1787.

Return with joy . . . to the Constitution? TJ to Elias Shipman, July 12, 1801.

Every honest man . . . rail without intermission: TJ to Dr. Benjamin Rush, December 20, 1801.

Our part is . . . be with us: TJ to General James Breckenridge, April 9, 1822.

I sincerely believe . . . the bodily deformities: TJ to Thomas Law, July 13, 1814.

I shall expect . . . commit an error: TJ to Colonel Edward Carrington, March 3, 1781.

It is not . . . its real author: TJ to John Norvell, June 11, 1807.

Where wrong has . . . censurable as such: Minutes as Rector of the University of Virginia of a Meeting Held on October 3, 1825.

The right of . . . difference of opinion: TJ to Elbridge Gerry, March 29, 1801.

For even if . . . basis of esteem: TJ to Elbridge Gerry, January 26, 1799.

SIMPLICITY

I am for . . . frugal and simple: TJ to Elbridge Gerry, January 26, 1799.

The accounts of . . . by common farmers: TJ to James Madison, March 6, 1796.

The people through . . . and civil freedom: TJ to Edward Livingston, April 30, 1800.

Our predecessors have . . . organized at first: TJ to Albert Gallatin, April 1, 1802.

Let us deserve . . . patronage, and irresponsibility: Ibid.

Congress will pretty . . . form of government: TJ to General Thaddeus Kosciusko, April 2, 1802.

The Senate and . . . would follow them: TJ to William Carmichael, August 9, 1789.

I served with . . . follow of themselves: Autobiography, 1821.

Speeches of sententious . . . with the hour: TJ to David Harding, April 20, 1824.

In style, I . . . brevity, and simplicity: TJ to George Wythe (Note E to Autobiography), November 1, 1778.

No style of . . . an unnecessary one: TJ to Thomas Jefferson Randolph, December 7, 1808.

No writer has . . . by Dr. Franklin: TJ to Francis Eppes, January 19, 1821.

I thought it . . . the lawyers themselves: Autobiography, 1821.

Let things come . . . of any artifices: TJ to Governor James Monroe, April 13, 1800.

Honest simplicity is . . . of being cherished: Travelling Notes for Mr. Rutledge and Mr. Shippen, June 3, 1788.

I long to . . . of the wise: TJ to Martha Jefferson Randolph, January 26, 1801.

I had rather . . . power can give: TJ to Alexander Donald, February 7, 1788.

LIVING IN THE PRESENT

Our business is . . . on the globe: TJ to Governor George Clinton, December 31, 1803.

It can never . . . and ourselves united: Notes on the State of Virginia, 1782.

I am greatly . . . our respectability abroad: TJ to John Brown, May 26, 1788.

The ground of . . . yet to get: TJ to the Reverend Charles Clay, January 27, 1790.

Although our prospect . . . resources are competent: TJ to James Bowdoin, July 10, 1806.

It is our . . . as one man: TJ to James Lewis, May 9, 1798.

I agree in . . . than the remedy: Reports and Opinions as Secretary of State, June 3, 1790: Opinion Regarding the Debts Due the Soldiers of Virginia and North Carolina.

That our Creator . . . can move something: TJ to Thomas Earle, September 24, 1823.

Let us draw . . . for the living: TJ to Monsieur Pierre Jean Georges Cabanis, July 12, 1803.

Rights and powers . . . rights of man: TJ to Major John Cartwright, June 5, 1824.

Of the public . . . time for recording: TJ to Horatio G. Spafford, May 11, 1819.

Our duty is . . . they may be: Sixth Annual Message to Congress, December 2, 1806.

Never put off . . . can do today: TJ to Thomas Jefferson Smith, February 21, 1825.

I hope you . . . a bad thing: TJ to Martha Jefferson, December 11, 1783.

Nature will not . . . omissions of this: TJ to Joseph C. Cabell, January 31, 1821.

There is a . . . of all mankind: TJ to Archibald Thweat, January 19, 1821.

ENTHUSIASM

A rising nation ... of the undertaking: First Inaugural Address, March 4, 1801.

We contemplate this ... above all price: First Annual Message to Congress, December 8, 1801.

As the storm ... it was tried: TJ to Dr. Joseph Priestley, March 21, 1801.

We shall have ... ignorance and barbarism: TJ to John Adams, August 1, 1816.

The preservation of ... of the globe: TJ to Reverend Samuel Knox, February 12, 1810.

The work we ... canvas we begin: TJ to William Dunbar, May 12, 1805.

I rejoice when ... shaped for them: TJ to Judge John Tyler, June 18, 1804.

Although I do ... to be effected: TJ to Monsieur Pierre Samuel du Pont de Nemours, April 24, 1816.

Seven years ago ... weakening powers can: TJ to Edward Livingston, March 25, 1825.

I have often ... a young gardener: TJ to Charles W. Peale, August 20, 1811.

Botany I rank ... for our bodies: TJ to Dr. Thomas Cooper, October 7, 1814.

There is not ... anything that moves: TJ to Martha Jefferson Randolph, December 23, 1790.

The motion of ... hours and actions: TJ to James Madison, June 9, 1793.

PATRIOTISM

We are trusted ... hope and happiness: Reply to Public Address: To the Citizens of Washington, March 4, 1809.

My earnest prayers ... all minor passions: TJ to John Hollins, May 5, 1811.

To preserve the ... hostile to both: Reply to Public Address: To the General Assembly of Rhode Island and Providence Plantations, May 26, 1801.

The first object ... my own country: TJ to Elbridge Gerry, January 26, 1799.

the asylum for ... great and good: TJ to Dr. Joseph Priestley, January 27, 1800.

In that is ... friendly to us: TJ to Elbridge Gerry, January 26, 1799.

There is not ... more sacred respect: TJ to Maria Cosway, October 12, 1786.

where the virtues ... to be weakened: TJ to Peter Carr, August 10, 1787.

A character of ... to an individual: Notes on a Conversation with Dawson, January 25, 1808.

A nation, as ... for his society: TJ to George Hammond, May 29, 1792.

The man who ... of warding off: TJ to Elbridge Gerry, June 21, 1797.

To no events . . . calamities my affliction: Reply to Public Address: To the
Legislature of the State of Georgia, February 3, 1809.

Nothing on earth . . . our country, however: Appeal to the Virginia Legislature for
a Lottery on His Lands, February 1826.

Our fellow citizens . . . in our affections: TJ to Dr. James Mease, September 26,
1825.

Even should the . . . who work them: TJ to John Adams, September 12, 1821.

Looking forward with . . . prosperity and happiness: Eighth Annual Message to
Congress, November 8, 1808.

God send to . . . a happy deliverance: TJ to John Taylor, February 14, 1821.

LIBERTY

Every man, and . . . society of men: Opinion on the Question Whether the
President Should Veto the Bill, Declaring That the Seat of Government
Shall Be Transferred to the Potomac in the Year 1790, July 15, 1790.

All, too, will . . . and one mind: First Inaugural Address, March 4, 1801.

In every government . . . a certain degree: Notes on the State of Virginia, 1782.

I consider the . . . persons administering it: Opinion on the Question Whether
the United States Have a Right to Renounce Their Treaties with France,
or Hold Them Suspended, April 23, 1793.

It should be . . . but moral law: TJ to Judge Spencer Roane, September 6,
1819.

The equal rights . . . of his country: TJ to Monsieur Adamantios Coray,
October 31, 1823.

What has destroyed . . . a Venetian senate: TJ to Joseph C. Cabell, February 2, 1816.

Indeed, it is . . . whole United States: TJ to Mrs. Elizabeth Trist, August 18, 1785.

Our lot has . . . of his tyrants: TJ to Monsieur François de Barbé-Marbois,
June 14, 1817.

If ever this . . . spread of surface: TJ to William T. Barry, July 2, 1822.

The time to . . . shall have entered: Notes on the State of Virginia, 1782.

I have much . . . open to them: TJ to Monsieur François de Barbé-Marbois,
June 14, 1817.

I considered as . . . rights of self-government: TJ to John Jacob Astor, May 24, 1812.

We should have . . . empire and self-government: TJ to James Madison, April 27,
1809.

We exist, and . . . one of force: TJ to Richard Rush, October 20, 1820.

It is indeed . . . triumphantly through them: TJ to William Hunter, March 11, 1790.

I join with . . . of the globe: TJ to John Dickinson, March 6, 1801.

In Turkey, where . . . of our liberty: TJ to James Madison, December 20, 1787.

The way to . . . for the best: TJ to Joseph C. Cabell, February 2, 1816.

The article nearest . . . of the people: TJ to Samuel Kercheval, September 5, 1816.

To preserve the . . . profusion and servitude: TJ to Samuel Kercheval, July 12, 1816.

Considering the general . . . instituted to guard: First Annual Message to Congress, December 8, 1801.

To take from . . . acquired by it": TJ to Joseph Milligan, April 6, 1816.

A bill of . . . laws of nations: TJ to James Madison, December 20, 1787.

You seem to . . . co-sovereign within themselves: TJ to William Charles Jarvis, September 28, 1820.

In every country . . . for their purposes: TJ to Horatio G. Spafford, March 17, 1814.

History, I believe . . . their own purposes: TJ to Baron Alexander von Humboldt, December 6, 1813.

I have sworn . . . mind of man: TJ to Dr. Benjamin Rush, September 23, 1800.

Rebellion to tyrants is obedience to God: Motto on Jefferson's Seal.

The eyes of . . . fire of liberty: TJ to John Hollins, May 5, 1811.

I hope and . . . rights of man: TJ to Benjamin Galloway, February 2, 1812.

May the Declaration . . . security of self-government: TJ to Roger C. Weightman, June 24, 1826.

Cherish every measure . . . over the globe: TJ to Edward Livingston, April 4, 1824.

DREAMING THE IMPOSSIBLE

Our Revolution commenced . . . on our hearts: TJ to Major John Cartwright, June 5, 1824.

Ours was not . . . of every citizen: TJ to John Hambden Pleasants, April 19, 1824.

Our lot has . . . of the laws: Reply to Address: To the Democratic-Republicans from the Townships of Washington County, Pennsylvania, March 31, 1809.

But the sufferings . . . or less free: TJ to Mrs. Elizabeth Trist, April 28, 1816.

A first attempt . . . even of heaven: TJ to John Adams, September 4, 1823.

In every country . . . bright and serene: TJ to Benjamin Waring, March 23, 1801.

I have observed . . . from the earth: TJ to William Ludlow, September 6, 1824.

All eyes are . . . grace of God: TJ to Roger C. Weightman, June 24, 1826.

Mine, after all . . . and future times: TJ to José Francisco Correa de Serra, November 25, 1817.

ONENESS

We feel that . . . its individual members: TJ to Dr. Joseph Priestley, June 19, 1802.

Our true interest . . . depends our happiness: TJ to James Monroe, August 11, 1786.

I sincerely wish . . . of the whole: TJ to Hugh Williamson, February 11, 1798.

It will be . . . of effecting it: TJ to Elbridge Gerry, March 29, 1801.

The good sense . . . its proper point: TJ to Marquis de Lafayette, October 28, 1822.

The cement of . . . immovable a basis: TJ to Marquis de Lafayette, February 14, 1815.

By bringing the . . . reason, and morality: TJ to Dr. Thomas Cooper, November 2, 1822.

The greatest good . . . them one people: TJ to John Dickinson, July 23, 1801.

Their arts, their . . . vice and violence: TJ to Colonel William Duane, August 4, 1812.

I sincerely pray . . . liberty, and happiness: Reply to Address: To Messrs. Thomas, Ellicot, and others, November 13, 1807.

Every human being . . . of every other: TJ to Chevalier Luis de Onis, April 28, 1814.

If it be . . . being on earth: TJ to James Monroe, July 11, 1801.

The moral doctrines . . . and common aids: Syllabus of an Estimate of the Merit of the Doctrines of Jesus, Compared with Those of Others, April 1803. Sent to Dr. Benjamin Rush, April 21, 1803.

No doctrines of Jesus lead to schism: TJ to Dr. Ezra Stiles, June 25, 1819.

We are all . . . ought to do?: Indian Addresses: To the Brothers of the Delaware and Shawanee Nations, February 10, 1802.

In that branch . . . do not differ: TJ to Dr. Ezra Stiles, June 25, 1819.

He who steadily . . . they all differ: TJ to William Canby, September 18, 1813.

On entering the . . . my earnest prayer: TJ to Miles King, September 26, 1814.

HOPE

We have acted . . . my constant prayer: TJ to the Members of the Baptist Church of Buck Mountain in Albemarle, April 13, 1809.

We are likely . . . attempted against us: TJ to Phillip Mazzei, April 24, 1796.

I will not . . . on steady advance: TJ to John Adams, September 12, 1821.

The spirit of . . . opened their eyes: TJ to Thomas Lomax, March 12, 1799.

Our experience so . . . wealth and force: Reply to Address: To Taber Fitch and Connecticut Republicans, November 21, 1808.

We shall never . . . arena of gladiators: TJ to Elbridge Gerry, May 13, 1797.

Here we are . . . follow our inclinations: TJ to William H. Cabell, November 1, 1807.

I hope we . . . to procure it: TJ to Samuel Adams, March 29, 1801.

I indulge a . . . the local governments: TJ to General Samuel Smith, May 3, 1823.

To promote, therefore . . . and philanthropic work: TJ to F. A. Van der Kemp, March 22, 1812.

We, too, shall . . . better of them: TJ to Thomas Digges, July 1, 1806.

Should things go . . . their elective rights: TJ to Wilson C. Nicholas, April 13, 1806.

We are sincerely . . . present abject condition: TJ to Thomas Cooper, November 29, 1802.

The light which . . . its inevitable crush: TJ to Marquis de Lafayette, December 26, 1820.

The ball of . . . round the globe: TJ to Tench Coxe, June 1, 1795.

That every man . . . an infinite degree: TJ to Cornelius Camden Blatchley, October 21, 1822.

Nature has sown . . . for their cultivation: Act for the Establishment of Elementary Schools, Sent to Joseph C. Cabell, September 9, 1817.

The reformation of . . . the like offenses: Bill for Proportioning Crimes and Punishments, Sent to George Wythe, November 1, 1778.

I had rather . . . roughness of life: TJ to Maria Cosway, October 12, 1786.

My theory has . . . gloom of despair: TJ to Monsieur François de Barbé-Marbois, June 14, 1817.

When I contemplate... burners of witches: TJ to Benjamin Waterhouse, March 3, 1818.

Withdrawn by age... of a visit: TJ to Judge Augustus B. Woodward, April 3, 1825.

I like the... of the past: TJ to John Adams, August 1, 1816.

That yourself, your... and holy keeping: Letter written to Louis XVI at the order of George Washington, and signed by the latter, March 14, 1792.

LIFE ACCEPTANCE

The varieties in... standard of uniformity: TJ to James Fishback, September 27, 1809.

I see too... we would wish: TJ to John Randolph, December 1, 1803.

I do not... would be uppermost: TJ to Mann Page, August 30, 1795.

Ignorance and bigotry... incapable of self-government: TJ to Marquis de Lafayette, May 14, 1817.

An association of... or a vestry: TJ to John Taylor, June 1, 1798.

It seems that... by local passions: TJ to Governor Robert Williams, November 1, 1807.

It is very... not follow us: TJ to John Wilson, August 17, 1813.

If we keep... tempests, earthquakes, etc.: TJ to Thomas W. Maury, January 27, 1816.

The most fortunate... it has fallen: TJ to John Page, July 15, 1763.

My principle is... disposal of them: TJ to Dr. George Logan, October 3, 1813.

Deeply practiced in... same wound himself?: TJ to Maria Cosway, October 12, 1786.

To the question... are to drink: TJ to John Adams, August 1, 1816.

The injury of... very confined motion: TJ to Dr. James Currie, August 4, 1787.

We have no... who gives them: TJ to Maria Cosway, October 12, 1786.

Man, like the... and unsightly appendage: TJ to General Henry Dearborn, August 17, 1821.

There is a... right to advance: TJ to Dr. Benjamin Rush, August 17, 1811.

I am now... peace, and goodwill: TJ to Samuel Kercheval, July 12, 1816.

Dr. Franklin used... time for anything: TJ to Abigail Adams, August 22, 1813.

Our machines have... within that period: TJ to John Adams, July 5, 1814.

I wish to... on the post: TJ to Judge Spencer Roane, September 6, 1819.

When you and . . . the great majority": TJ to Governor John Page, June 25, 1804.

SELF-GIVING

We acknowledge that . . . charges of infancy: TJ to John W. Eppes, September 11, 1813.

God has formed . . . value our own: TJ to Miles King, September 26, 1814.

I believe that . . . contrary in another: TJ to John Adams, October 14, 1816.

What more sublime . . . with one another: TJ to Maria Cosway, October 12, 1786.

I deem it . . . it is capable: TJ to Drs. Rogers and Slaughter, March 2, 1806.

Take more pleasure . . . will love you: TJ to Mary Jefferson, April 11, 1790.

We should all . . . eschewers of evil: TJ to Dr. Ezra Stiles, June 25, 1809.

A nation, by . . . of mere money: Special Presidential Message, January 13, 1806.

My public proceedings . . . of our country: TJ to Dr. Elijah Griffith, May 28, 1809.

I had no . . . the public satisfaction: TJ to President George Washington, December 15, 1789.

I preferred public . . . all personal considerations: TJ to John W. Eppes, September 11, 1813.

and retired much . . . the public service: TJ to Edward Rutledge, December 27, 1796.

If, in the . . . its full reward: TJ to David Barrow, May 1, 1815.

I came of . . . in other States: Appeal to the Virginia Legislature for a Lottery of His Lands, February 1826.

I have done . . . to my country: Last spoken words, July 4, 1826.

FORGIVENESS

In little disputes . . . trifles in dispute: TJ to Francis Eppes, May 21, 1816.

Try to let . . . yours to be: TJ to Mary Jefferson, April 11, 1790.

It is useless . . . our old accounts: TJ to Anne Cary Randolph, July 6, 1805.

Harmony in the . . . it is complete: TJ to Mary Jefferson, January 7, 1798.

In stating prudential . . . by suggesting doubts: TJ to Thomas Jefferson Randolph, November 24, 1808.

When I hear . . . he prefers error: Ibid.

I tolerate with . . . its different results: TJ to Abigail Adams, September 11, 1804.

Cruel and sanguinary . . . the laws observed: Bill for Proportioning Crimes and Punishments, Sent to George Wythe, November 1, 1778.

It may be . . . has taken place: Notes on the State of Virginia, 1782.

Treasons, taking the . . . punished by exile: Report on Convention with Spain, March 22, 1792.

I shall often . . . freedom of all: First Inaugural Address, March 4, 1801.

It is an . . . will get tamed: TJ to Martha Jefferson Randolph, January 26, 1801.

If we can . . . has conciliated many: TJ to William B. Giles, March 23, 1801.

There are no . . . attention or skill: TJ to Josephus B. Stuart, May 10, 1817.

I cannot have . . . of every measure: Eighth Annual Message to Congress, November 8, 1808.

For honest errors . . . may be hoped: Speech to U.S. Senate, February 28, 1801.

LOVE

I feel extraordinary . . . of the heart: TJ to Governor John Henry, December 31, 1797.

It has been . . . his political opinions: TJ to Richard M. Johnson, March 10, 1808.

I hope that . . . heal these also: TJ to John Hollins, May 5, 1811.

One side fears . . . first withdraw himself: TJ to Abigail Adams, September 11, 1804.

Your principles and . . . of our acquaintance: TJ to General Thaddeus Kosciusko, June 1, 1798.

May heaven favor . . . pour its favors: TJ to Monsieur de Lafayette, June 16, 1792.

I am happy . . . bought too dear: TJ to Martha Jefferson Randolph, May 8, 1791.

Let us come . . . bright and clear: Indian Addresses: To the Wolf and People of the Mandan Nations, December 30, 1806.

Friendship is precious . . . life is sunshine: TJ to Maria Cosway, October 12, 1786.

An honest heart . . . is the second: TJ to Peter Carr, August 19, 1785.

Lose no moment . . . heart in benevolence: TJ to Martha Jefferson, March 6, 1786.

Be you the . . . that of others: TJ to Martha Jefferson Randolph, July 17, 1790.

My hand denies . . . few esteemed characters: TJ to Mrs. Elizabeth Trist, December 15, 1786.

Friendship is like ... and restorative cordial: TJ to Dr. Benjamin Rush,
    August 17, 1811.
I find as ... I loved first: TJ to Mrs. Mary Bolling, July 23, 1787.
The friendship which ... my last affections: TJ to James Madison, February 17,
    1826.
I am sure ... of it yourself: TJ to John Adams, August 15, 1820.
If to the ... under my regard: TJ to Thomas Jefferson Grotjan, January 10,
    1824.

PATIENCE
Let no proof ... patience or acquiesence: TJ to Martha Jefferson Randolph,
    July 17, 1790.
Much better, if ... the subject together: TJ to Mary Jefferson Eppes, January 7,
    1798.
Go on then ... to render habitual: TJ to Mary Jefferson, May 30, 1791.
In truth, politeness ... will of another!: TJ to Thomas Jefferson Randolph,
    November 24, 1808.
Take things always by their smooth handle: TJ to Thomas Jefferson Smith,
    February 21, 1825.
Never be angry ... harm of them: TJ to Mary Jefferson, April 11, 1790.
Anger only serves ... alienate their esteem: TJ to Martha Jefferson, April 7, 1787.
When angry, count ... angry, an hundred: TJ to Thomas Jefferson Smith,
    February 21, 1825.
Setting aside the ... of the Atlantic: TJ to John W. Eppes, September 29, 1811.
Acquiescence under wrong ... want, and wretchedness: TJ to James Madison,
    March 23, 1815.
I feared from ... success in it: TJ to John Adams, January 22, 1821.
More than a ... or the one: TJ to the Marquis de Lafayette, February 14, 1815.
A little patience ... its true principles: TJ to John Taylor, June 4, 1798.
We must have ... chapter of accidents: TJ to William B. Giles, December 26,
    1825.
Patience will bring all to rights: TJ to General Horatio Gates, May 30, 1797.
and steady perseverance ... the blessed end: TJ to General James Breckenridge,
    April 9, 1822.

SELF-DISCIPLINE

Whenever you feel . . . under all circumstances: TJ to Francis Eppes, May 21, 1816.

The prudence and . . . befriends rational conclusion: First Annual Message to Congress, December 8, 1801.

Strive to be . . . all living creatures: TJ to Martha Jefferson, November 28, 1783.

Never trouble another . . . can do yourself: TJ to Thomas Jefferson Smith, February 21, 1825.

Remote from all . . . lean on others: TJ to Martha Jefferson, March 28, 1787.

Dependence begets subservience . . . designs of ambition: Notes on the State of Virginia, 1782.

Take any race . . . and no mind: TJ to Governor John Langdon, March 5, 1810.

In a world . . . against all mankind: TJ to Martha Jefferson, May 21, 1787.

Never buy what . . . you have it: TJ to Thomas Jefferson Smith, February 21, 1825.

We shall all . . . of the majority: TJ to John W. Eppes, September 11, 1813.

Having seen the . . . prosperity and happiness: TJ to Henry Middleton, January 8, 1813.

If there be . . . do with conquest: TJ to William Short, July 28, 1791.

The energies of . . . characterize this commonwealth: TJ to Messrs. Eddy, Russell, Thurber, Wheaton, and Smith, March 27, 1801.

Friendly nations always . . . differences in private: Note of Cabinet Meeting on Edmond Charles Genet, August 2, 1793.

I hope our . . . it will be: TJ to Thomas Leiper, June 12, 1815.

I was a . . . a hard student: TJ to Dr. Vine Utley, March 21, 1819.

Our projected college . . . not a little: TJ to John Adams, September 8, 1817.

We studiously avoid . . . for their institution: TJ to Ellen W. Coolidge, August 27, 1825.

We have spent . . . it is free: TJ to Dr. Joseph Willard, March 24, 1789.

NOT FEARING LOSS

To procure tranquility . . . Fear. 4. Deceit: TJ to William Short, October 31, 1819.

Never throw off . . . should sink yourself: TJ to Martha Jefferson Randolph, April 28, 1793.

Never fear the . . . employment in it: TJ to Peter Carr, June 22, 1792.

I am not . . . truth and science: TJ to Dr. John Manners, February 22, 1814.

Here, where all . . . which offers good: TJ to John Waldo, August 16, 1813.

I am not . . . for continued freedom: TJ to Samuel Kercheval, July 12, 1816.

The cherishment of . . . the other party: TJ to Judge William Johnson, June 12, 1823.

It is not . . . differences by duel: TJ to James Ogilvie, June 23, 1806.

Let those flatter . . . an American art: Summary View of the Rights of British America, 1774.

I never had . . . afraid to own: TJ to Francis Hopkinson, March 13, 1789.

I fear no . . . action with me: Notes on a Conversation with Burr, April 15, 1806.

As to federal . . . notice from myself: TJ to Dr. George Logan, June 20, 1816.

You ask, if . . . in the stern: TJ to John Adams, April 8, 1816.

SILENCE

Wars and contentions . . . my own country: TJ to Count Diodati, March 29, 1807.

From a very . . . a single instance: TJ to President George Washington, June 19, 1796.

In the election . . . of the public: Notes on a Conversation with Burr, January 26, 1804.

I shall pursue . . . path of right: TJ to General George Washington, April 16, 1784.

The path we . . . on in happiness: TJ to Thomas Cooper, November 29, 1802.

The less that . . . necessary, in silence: TJ to Levi Lincoln, August 30, 1803.

I confess that . . . of receiving them: TJ to Governor James Sullivan, June 19, 1807.

I am sincerely . . . abhorrence of dispute: TJ to President George Washington, May 8, 1791.

My great wish . . . of my duty: TJ to Francis Hopkinson, March 13, 1789.

Long tried in . . . its only medicines: TJ to Governor W. C. C. Claiborne, May 3, 1810.

Be a listener . . . habit of silence: TJ to Thomas Jefferson Randolph, November 24, 1808.

I think one . . . he reflects more: TJ to John Bannister, June 19, 1787.

To every obstacle . . . and soothing language: TJ to William Short, March 18, 1792.

A firm, but . . . likely to succeed: TJ to John Jay, May 23, 1788.

We often repent . . . we have not: TJ to Gideon Granger, March 9, 1814.

Say nothing of . . . a bad one: TJ to John Adams, January 11, 1817.

Religion is not . . . Maker and ourselves: TJ to Thomas Leiper, January 21, 1809.

I have left . . . from their effects: TJ to Mrs. M. Harrison Smith, August 6, 1816.

TRUTH SEEKING

Be industrious in . . . your own happiness: TJ to Francis Wayles Eppes, September 6, 1811.

A patient pursuit . . . attain sure knowledge: Notes on the State of Virginia, 1782.

I am myself . . . than my facts: TJ to George F. Hopkins, September 5, 1822.

I am satisfied . . . have no evidence: TJ to John Adams, August 15, 1820.

Follow truth as . . . in endless succession: TJ to John Adams, December 10, 1819.

He who knows . . . falsehoods and errors: TJ to John Norvell, June 11, 1807.

It is always . . . what is wrong: TJ to Reverend James Madison, July 19, 1788.

No vice is . . . time so useless: TJ to Martha Jefferson, April 7, 1787.

Truth is the first object: TJ to Dr. James Mease, January 15, 1809.

Your reason is . . . of blindfolded fear: TJ to Peter Carr, August 10, 1787.

Almighty God hath . . . on reason alone: Virginia Statute for Religious Freedom, 1779.

The most effectual . . . of the people: Bill for the More General Diffusion of Knowledge, July 18, 1778.

It is an . . . truth and reason: TJ to Monsieur N. G. Dufief, April 19, 1814.

Light and liberty go together: TJ to Tench Coxe, June 1, 1795.

I look to . . . happiness of man: TJ to Cornelius Camden Blatchley, October 21, 1822.

Enlighten the people . . . dawn of day: TJ to Monsieur Pierre Samuel du Pont de Nemours, April 24, 1816.

If a nation . . . never will be: TJ to Colonel Charles Yancey, January 6, 1816.

No nation is . . . ignorance with impunity: Minutes as Rector of the University of Virginia, 1821.

Truth advances, and . . . to another step: TJ to Thomas Cooper, October 7, 1814.

Truth will do . . . minds of men: Notes on Religion, October 1776.

Truth is the . . . to contradict them: Virginia Statute for Religious Freedom, 1779.

Truth and reason ... will eternally prevail: TJ to Reverend Samuel Knox, February 12, 1810.

PEACE PRAYER

Peace is our passion: TJ to Sir John Sinclair, June 30, 1803.

I have ever ... an intimate connection: TJ to Dr. George Logan, October 3, 1813.

From the moment ... peace and justice: Reply to Public Address: To the Republicans of Georgetown, March 8, 1809.

Peace and justice ... the American societies: TJ to José Francisco Correa de Serra, October 24, 1820.

The happiness of ... pursuits of peace: Reply to Public Address: To the Young Republicans of Pittsburgh, December 2, 1808.

Our desire is ... surely to prosperity: TJ to George Hammond, May 15, 1793.

Go on in ... body of man: TJ to Thomas Paine, June 19, 1792.

Peace and friendship ... our wisest policy: TJ to C.W. F. Dumas, May 6, 1786.

I believe that ... of the former: TJ to James Monroe, June 28, 1793.

I abhor war ... scourge of mankind: TJ to Elbridge Gerry, May 13, 1797.

I love peace ... to the sufferer: TJ to Tench Coxe, May 1, 1794.

If nations go ... peace on earth: TJ to Madame de Staël, July 16, 1807.

We think that ... react on themselves: TJ to Monsieur Pierre Jean Georges Cabanis, July 12, 1803.

We have, therefore ... existing in it: TJ to General Thaddeus Kosciusko, April 13, 1811.

My hope is in peace: TJ to Monsieur José Francisco Correa de Serra, December 26, 1814.

Thanks be to ... continue in it: TJ to Count Antonio Dugnani, February 14, 1818.

It will be ... entirely without remuneration: TJ to Noah Worcester, November 26, 1817.

I hope we ... of the fighter: TJ to John Adams, June 1, 1822.

I wish that ... cultivated by all: TJ to Thomas Leiper, June 12, 1815.

My hope of ... friendship from others: TJ to the Earl of Buchan, July 10, 1803.

We, I hope ... race of peace: TJ to Monsieur Pierre Jean Georges Cabanis, July 12, 1803.

To preserve and . . . of my administration: Reply to Public Address: To the
  Members of the Baltimore Baptist Association, October 17, 1808.

Twenty years of . . . a peaceable nation: TJ to Monsieur Pierre Jean Georges
  Cabanis, July 12, 1803.

I pray for . . . see three wars: TJ to Thomas Leiper, July 12, 1815.

That peace, safety . . . lived in vain: TJ to Benjamin Waring, March 23, 1801.

Heaven bless you . . . elements into peace: TJ to Madame de Bréhan, October 9,
  1787.

Lord, now lettest . . . depart in peace: TJ's dying prayer, July 4, 1826.

ACKNOWLEDGMENTS

Light and Liberty benefited from the encouragement, efforts, and advice of many people, and I am pleased to acknowledge their contributions. My parents, Pete and Betty Petersen, built life foundations for their children on Jeffersonian principles. Three extraordinary teachers, Dick Skinner, Gloria Steinberg, and Professor Barry Karl, enriched a happy public-school and Brown University education. Each nourished a growing love of our country and its founding tenets. Sri Chinmoy, long an admirer of Thomas Jefferson and exemplar of living in Jefferson's spirit, encouraged me to add a spiritual perspective to my understanding of Jefferson and America's origins.

The enterprise was sustained by the generous goodwill of Merrill Peterson, the eminent scholar and biographer of Thomas Jefferson, and by the steady support of Dan Jordan, president of the Thomas Jefferson Foundation and guiding force in preserving Monticello as a world treasure. The distinguished writer Louis Auchincloss graced this arrangement of Jefferson's wisdom with an enthusiasm that helped carry the project to fruition. Special appreciation is due my agent, Martha Keys, David Ebershoff at Random House, and more than a few good friends, colleagues, and family members, each of whom heartened my progress with their fond regard for Jefferson.

The kind assistance of Sarah Pfeiffer, Marie Lellis, Susan Wales, Elizabeth Dunne Gartner, Lizette Martinos, and Debbie Arominski was vital in the development and processing of the text through innumerable drafts. Gratitude I offer most especially to my life's love, Kathy Rhodes, whose patient and cheerful acceptance of the demands of the undertaking made Thomas Jefferson a welcome and regular guest in our home.

About the Editor

ERIC S. PETERSEN is a managing partner at the New York City law firm of Hawkins Delafield & Wood LLP. Educated at Brown University and the University of Chicago Law School, he has studied Jefferson's life and works since 1993. He lives in Connecticut.

A NOTE ON THE TYPE

The principal text of this Modern Library edition
was set in a digitized version of Janson, a typeface that
dates from about 1690 and was cut by Nicholas Kis,
a Hungarian working in Amsterdam. The original matrices have
survived and are held by the Stempel foundry in Germany.
Hermann Zapf redesigned some of the weights and sizes for
Stempel, basing his revisions on the original design.